can't cook, want to learn

carolyn humphries

foulsham

LONDON • NEW YORK • TORONTO • SYDNEY

foulsham

The Publishing House, Bennetts Close, Cippenham,
Berkshire, SL1 5AP, England

ISBN 0-572-02514-9

Artwork by Sarah Wilkinson.

Printed in Great Britain by St. Edmundsbury Press, Bury St. Edmunds, Suffolk.

contents

1 all about this book

At last! A book that actually tells you not only what and how to cook but exactly when to cook it so that you produce perfect main meals with all the trimmings. Most cookery books you look at are full of technical jargon, complicated methods and lists of ingredients as long as your arm. What's more, they tell you to serve your masterpiece with umpteen vegetables and a sauce, but they don't explain how and when are you supposed to prepare them.

This book is designed for anyone and everyone who wants to prepare complete, everyday meals. It tells you exactly what you'll need, shows you how to prepare the ingredients and guides you step by step through the cooking method so that everything is ready to dish up all at the same time. There is no fuss and no frills, just your favourite meals – and many more besides – ready to be tackled with ease.

This book is about cooking, starting from scratch. So, in Your Storecupboard (see page 6), we show you how to build up a collection of useful ingredients you should keep in your kitchen cupboard, ready for whenever you want to make a meal. The list is intended only as a guide – you are bound to find other favourite items that you will want to add.

Most cookery books assume that you have some knowledge and experience of cooking. But not everyone does, so in this book we devote a whole section, Basic Cooking Skills (see page 8), to giving you step-by-step instructions on simple techniques that you will need to use over and over again.

Even with a recipe book in front of you, it is not always easy to understand exactly what is meant, especially if you are a bit hazy about cooking terminology; and a small mistake in a crucial stage can make a meal inedible. Our Notes on the Recipes (see page 7) provide you with some useful hints and tips to help you follow each recipe correctly. The section on Simple Food Hygiene (see page 5) gives you the essentials to follow to ensure healthy cooking and eating – make sure they become second nature too.

In the recipe section, each recipe is organised in the simplest possible way and includes everything you need to do to create a complete meal, in the order you will do it. So, no more getting to the last stage and finding you should have boiled the pasta 20 minutes earlier!

Once you have chosen your recipe, you will find that it contains two lists of ingredients: the first one includes items you will probably have in your storecupboard, and the second is a shopping list of extra ingredients and fresh produce you may need to buy. Make sure you assemble all these items before you start.

Of course, you will need some cookery equipment. There are dozens of kitchen utensils and appliances on the market, but only a small number of basic tools are really necessary. Make sure you always have the following to hand:

chopping board
sharp kitchen knives
scales
wooden spoons
fork, tablespoon and teaspoon
tongs
can opener
foil, kitchen paper (paper towels) and
    clingfilm (plastic wrap)
cups, plates, serving dishes and bowls

Where other items of special equipment are required in a recipe, you will find a reminder at the beginning.

In the final chapter, you will learn how to turn some of the recipes into impressive three-course meals with very little extra effort.

With all the help in this book, you will quickly learn just how easy it is to put complete meals together. Soon you will be confident enough to begin to experiment with your own ideas and discover how you can mix and match the basic elements of my recipes to create your own range of new meals. There really is no excuse any more for saying you can't cook.

2 simple food hygiene

A hygienic cook is a healthy cook and an unhygienic cook may make everyone ill – so please bear the following in mind.

Always wash your hands before preparing food.

Always wash and dry fresh produce before use.

Don't lick your fingers.

Don't keep tasting and stirring with the same spoon. Use a clean spoon every time you taste.

Never use a cloth to wipe down a dirty chopping board and then use the same one to wipe down your work surfaces – you will simply spread germs. Always wash your cloth well in hot, soapy water and, better still, use an anti-bacterial cleaner on all work surfaces and chopping boards as well.

Always transfer leftovers to a clean container and cover with a lid, clingfilm (plastic wrap) or foil. Leave until completely cold, then store in the fridge. Never put any warm food into the fridge.

Don't store raw and cooked meat on the same shelf in the fridge. Put raw meat on the bottom shelf, so it can't drip over other foods. Keep all perishable foods wrapped separately. Don't overfill the fridge or it won't maintain a low enough temperature.

When reheating food, always make sure it is piping hot throughout, never just lukewarm.

Don't re-freeze foods that have defrosted unless you cook them first. Never reheat previously cooked food more than once.

3 your storecupboard

It's a good idea to keep a selection of basic ingredients always to hand – it gives you more choice and it makes life much easier! However, there's no need to go out and buy everything on these lists. Build up your storecupboard gradually, to include your favourite items. Don't forget to replace them as you use them.

cans, jars, bottles and packets
tuna fish
corned beef
hot dog sausages
chopped tomatoes
carrots
sweetcorn (corn)
baked beans
pulses, including red kidney beans and lentils
fruit in natural juice, including pineapple rings
condensed soups: tomato and mushroom
condensed milk
evaporated milk
passata (sieved tomatoes)
caster (superfine) sugar
plain (all-purpose) flour
self-raising (self-rising) flour
cornflour (cornstarch)
shredded vegetable suet
baking powder
bicarbonate of soda (baking soda)
long-grain rice
pasta

dried fruit
sunflower or good-quality vegetable oil
olive oil
wine vinegar, red and white
lemon juice
clear honey
golden (light corn) syrup
black treacle (molasses)
jam (conserve)
marmalade
stuffing mix
flaked (slivered) almonds
desiccated (shredded) coconut
walnut pieces
toasted, chopped mixed nuts

herbs, spices, seasonings and flavourings
dried herbs, including oregano, basil, mint and mixed herbs and bouquet garni sachets
curry powder
spices: chilli powder, paprika; ground cinnamon, ginger, cumin and coriander (cilantro); grated nutmeg
dried onion granules
soy sauce
tomato ketchup (catsup)
pickles and chutneys
Worcestershire sauce
brown table sauce

horseradish sauce
tartare sauce
Tabasco sauce
salt and pepper, preferably black peppercorns in
    a grinder
mustard, preferably both English and Dijon
stock cubes: chicken, vegetable and beef
gravy block or browning
tube of tomato purée (paste)
tube of garlic purée

fridge
medium eggs
butter or margarine

milk
Cheddar cheese
tub of grated Parmesan cheese
mayonnaise
orange juice

freezer compartment
pastry (paste): shortcrust (basic pie crust), filo and
    puff
peas
chopped parsley
bread
ice cream

4 notes on the recipes

Always assemble your ingredients and equipment before you start.

Ingredients are given in metric, imperial and American measures. Use only one set per recipe.

American terms are given in brackets.

All can sizes are approximate – they differ slightly from brand to brand. For example, if the recipe calls for 400 g/14 oz/1 large can of chopped tomatoes and yours is a 413 g can – that's fine.

When a tablespoonful or teaspoonful of an ingredient is called for, ideally you should use cookery measuring spoons; level off the ingredient in the spoon to get an accurate measure. Ordinary spoons can be used, although

you may find you have to add a little more.

Purées (pastes), such as garlic and tomato, are very concentrated and should be used with caution as their flavours may completely overpower a dish. If a squeeze of garlic purée is called for, start with about 1 cm/½ in; a squeeze of tomato purée should be about 1 tablespoonful. Remember, all flavourings are a matter of preference, so taste your dish when it is cooked and then add more as you like.

Use medium eggs unless otherwise stated.

Preparation and cooking times are approximate.

Most recipes are for four servings. Just halve or double all the quantities as necessary.

5 basic cooking skills

Like so many things, cooking is very simple when you know how. So this section shows you, step by step, exactly how to master some of the basic skills and methods you will use over and over again when you are preparing a meal.

Every time you need to use one of these techniques for a recipe in this book, you'll find an arrow (➡) directing you to a visual reminder. The page reference shows you where to find the instructions. The step number relates back to the method point in the recipe. Of course, once you've used them a few times, you'll know just what to do without having to look it up!

separating an egg

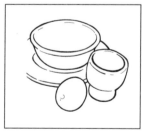

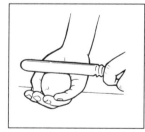

1 You will need a saucer, an egg cup and a small bowl.

2 Crack the shell of the egg by tapping sharply in the middle with a knife.

3 Holding the two halves of the shell over the saucer, gently pull them apart so that the contents fall on the saucer.

4 Invert an egg cup over the yolk and press firmly on to the saucer. Pick up the saucer and drain off the white into the small bowl.

chopping an onion

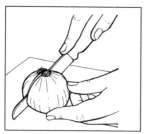  

1 Cut the point off the top of the onion. Pull off all the outer skin, leaving the root intact (this will help stop you crying). Cut the onion in half lengthways through the root.

2 Hold one half between your thumb and fingers, flat side down on a board, and slice at intervals from the root end to the tip.

3 Now turn the onion so that you can slice across the first set of cuts. Discard the root end. To chop finely, make the cuts closer together in both directions. To chop coarsely, make the cuts wider apart.

slicing an onion into rings

1 Don't peel the onion. Hold it firmly between your thumb and middle finger, with the root end in your hand.

2 Cut into fairly thin slices, starting at the tip end. When you get to the root end, discard it.

3 Peel off the brown outer layer and the next layer, if it seems tough, from each slice.

4 Separate the slices into rings. Cut the slices in half if you don't want rings.

dicing vegetables

1 Peel thinly with a potato peeler or sharp knife, if necessary.

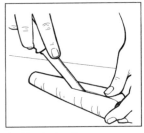

2 Cut in half lengthways.

3 Hold between your thumb and middle finger and cut into strips.

4 Turn the vegetable, still holding it firmly together, and cut at right angles to the first cuts. For larger dice, make the cuts wider apart. For smaller dice, make them closer together.

boiling potatoes and root vegetables

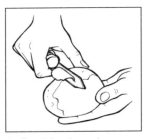

1 Peel thinly with a potato peeler or sharp vegetable knife, or scrape, or scrub, as necessary.

2 Cut into even-sized pieces. Leave baby new potatoes or carrots whole. Place in a pan with just enough cold water to cover all the vegetable pieces and add a very little salt.

3 Cover with a lid and bring up to the boil over a high heat. When the water is bubbling, turn the heat down so that the vegetables boil gently. Leave to cook until they feel tender when a knife is inserted in them – anything from 5 to 15 minutes.

4 Tip carefully into a colander in the sink to drain.

making chips (fries)

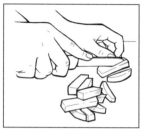

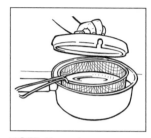

1 Wash or scrub the potatoes (don't peel them unless you want to). Cut each one into four thick slices, then cut the slices into strips to make chips. Wrap in a clean tea towel (dish cloth) to dry.

2 Pour about 2.5 cm/ 1 in oil into a deep frying pan (skillet) and heat until your hand feels hot when held 5 cm/2 in above the surface.

3 Slide the chips gently down a fish slice into the pan (to prevent splashing) and allow to cook until golden, turning them occasionally. Drain on kitchen paper (paper towels).

NOTE: If you have a deep-fat fryer, follow the manufacturer's instructions.

cooking green leafy vegetables

1 Pull or cut off any outer, damaged leaves. Separate into leaves, discarding any thick stalks. Whole cabbage may be cut in half and the thick stalk removed. Rinse in cold water and drain.

2 Cut the leaves into pieces or thin shreds as appropriate.

3 Put about 2.5 cm/1 in water in a saucepan with a good pinch of salt. Heat until it is boiling rapidly. Add the greens and push down well as they begin to soften. Boil over a high heat until they are just tender but still have some texture. This will take 3–5 minutes.

4 Drain in a colander.

making a mixed salad

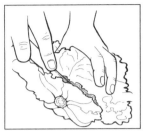

1 Choose a selection of differently coloured salad stuffs such as lettuce, tomatoes, cucumber, onion and green, yellow or red (bell) pepper.

2 Cut the root off the lettuce and separate into leaves. Wash, pat dry on kitchen paper (paper towels), then tear into pieces.

3 Slice the cucumber. Halve the tomatoes, then cut them into wedges.

4 Cut slices off an unpeeled onion, then separate into rings, discarding the outer tough skin and first layer (see Slicing an Onion into Rings page 9).

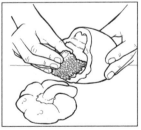

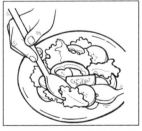

5 Cut a slice off the top of a pepper and pull out the core, seeds and any white membranes. Cut the pepper into thin rings.

6 Put all the ingredients into a salad bowl. Add a little French Dressing (see page 13), then, using salad servers or a large spoon and fork gently turn the vegetables over in the dressing until it is all glistening.

MAKING A GREEN SALAD:

Prepare as for mixed salad but use all green salad stuffs. Add other ingredients, such as avocado, peeled and

diced; canned artichoke hearts, drained and quartered; chopped celery sticks; watercress – anything you like, as long as it's green!

making french dressing

1 Quarter-fill a small, clean screw-topped jar with red or white wine vinegar.

2 Top up to three-quarters with olive oil. Add a good pinch of caster (superfine) sugar, a pinch of salt and some pepper.

3 Screw on the lid and shake thoroughly. Store in the fridge and use as required. Shake well before use.

NOTE: for extra flavour, try adding a squeeze of garlic purée (paste), or 1 tsp Dijon mustard or a good pinch of dried mixed herbs, tarragon or oregano to the basic mixture.

making garlic bread

1 Turn on the oven to 190°C/375°F/gas mark 5. Cut a small French stick into 12 slices but take care not to cut right through the bottom crust.

2 Using a table knife, mash 75 g/3 oz/⅓ cup butter or margarine with a small squeeze of garlic purée (paste) or more, if you like, on a small plate or saucer.

3 Spread this mixture between the slices and if there is any left over, spread it on top of the loaf.

4 Wrap in a piece of foil, shiny side in, making sure the loaf is completely covered. Bake in the oven for 15 minutes until the bread feels crisp on the outside and soft in the middle when squeezed. (Wear an oven glove!)

making a basic white sauce

1 Put 45 ml/3 tbsp plain (all-purpose) flour in a small saucepan.

2 Using a balloon whisk and stirring all the time, gradually add 300 ml/ ½ pt/1¼ cups milk until the mixture is smooth.

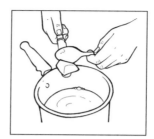

3 Add a knob of butter or margarine and a sprinkling of salt and pepper.

4 Cook over a fairly high heat, stirring with the whisk all the time, until the mixture is thick and bubbling. Continue to cook the sauce for 2 minutes. Use as required.

cooking rice

1 Three-quarters fill a large pan with water and add 1 tsp salt. Put over a high heat, cover with a lid and leave it until it is boiling. Meanwhile, measure the rice. Allow 50 g/2 oz/ ¼ cup per person.

2 Remove the pan lid. Pour the rice in a thin stream into the boiling water and stir well to separate the grains. Do not cover the pan again. Leave to boil for the time directed on the packet. Meanwhile, boil a kettle of water.

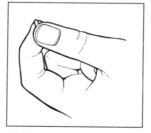

3 To test if the rice is cooked, lift out a few grains with a draining spoon and either taste or pinch a grain between your thumb and index finger. It should feel almost soft but still have some texture.

4 Place a colander in the sink and pour in the contents of the pan. Pour boiling water over the grains to rinse off excess starch, then lift up the colander and place on top of the saucepan to drain. Stir gently with a fork, then serve.

cooking spaghetti (or any other pasta)

1 Three-quarters fill a large pan with water and add 1 tsp salt and 1 tbsp oil. (This will stop it boiling over and prevent the pasta from being sticky.) Put over a high heat, cover with a lid and leave it to come to the boil.

2 While you wait, measure out the spaghetti. Allow 50–75 g/2–3 oz per person. When the water boils, remove the lid.

3 Hold the saucepan handle with one hand and the spaghetti with the other. Put the spaghetti into the water so that the ends touch the base of the pan.

4 Gently push the strands. They will gradually curl round the pan as they soften. Do not push too hard or they will snap. Once submerged, stir gently to separate the strands. Cook for the time directed on the packet. Do not cover the pan.

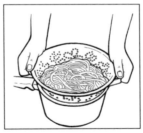

5 To test the spaghetti is cooked, lift a strand out of the pan and throw it at the wall – it will stick if it is cooked. (Don't forget to remove it!) Alternatively, just bite a strand. It should feel just soft but still with a little bit of chewiness to it.

6 Put a colander in the sink. Pour the contents of the saucepan into the colander and allow it to drain well.

7 Lift up the colander of spaghetti and place on top of the saucepan to finish draining while you get out the plates.

NOTE: Cook other pasta in exactly the same way but simply add it slowly to the boiling water, rather than feeding it in gradually. Allow 50 g/ 2 oz per person. Stir well to separate before cooking.

6 fry-ups

Frying (sautéing) is a great way of cooking things really quickly. Use the minimum of oil, butter or margarine and always drain chips (fries) or other crisp-fried foods on kitchen paper (paper towels) to remove any excess oil before serving.

the great british fry-up
for breakfast or brunch

SERVES 4

storecupboard ingredients

400 g/14 oz/1 large can of baked beans or tomatoes

sunflower oil

tomato ketchup (catsup) or brown table sauce

salt and pepper

2 slices of bread

4 eggs

shopping list

8 rashers (slices) of rindless back bacon

4 large or 8 small sausages OR 8 slices of black pudding

100 g/4 oz button mushrooms

extra equipment

small saucepan

medium saucepan

large frying pan (skillet)

fish slice

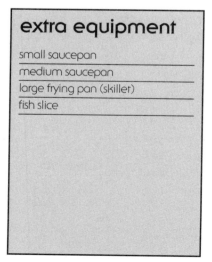

1   Turn on the oven at the lowest setting and put a large serving platter and plates in to warm.

2   Wipe the mushrooms to remove any soil. Place in a small saucepan with 4 tbsp water and a little salt and pepper. Bring to the boil over a high heat. Turn the heat down low, cover with a lid and leave to cook for 5 minutes.

3   While the mushrooms are cooking, empty the beans or tomatoes into a medium saucepan and put over a low heat to heat through, stirring occasionally with a wooden spoon.

4   Heat a frying pan, add the sausages and dry-fry over a fairly high heat until they are brown all over, turning frequently with a fish slice or tongs. Transfer to the large platter in the oven. If you are cooking black pudding, put a little oil in the frying pan and cook for 2 minutes on each side. Wipe out the pan before continuing with the rest of the cooking.

5   Add the bacon to the pan and cook until its fat is turning golden, turning over once. Transfer to the large platter in the oven.

6   Cut the bread slices into halves. Pour enough oil into the frying pan to cover the base. Heat until your hand feels hot when held 5 cm/2 in above it. Add the bread and fry (sauté) until brown underneath. Turn over with the fish slice and brown the other sides. Lift out of the pan, drain on kitchen paper (paper towels), then transfer to the large platter in the oven.

7   Heat a little more oil in the pan. Break the eggs into a cup, one at a time, and then gently slide into the hot oil. Cook the eggs until the whites are set and bubbling. Spoon a little of the hot oil over the yolks, if liked, to set the tops.

8   Carefully lift the eggs out of the pan on to the warmed plates with a fish slice. Divide the remaining fried ingredients between the plates and add the beans or tomatoes and mushrooms. Serve straight away with ketchup or brown table sauce.

leftovers fry-up
with vegetables and crusty bread

SERVES 4

storecupboard ingredients

400 g/14 oz/1 large can of baked beans

225 g/8 oz cooked, leftover meat (beef, lamb, pork or chicken)

350 g/12 oz cooked, leftover vegetables (any combination of carrots, cauliflower, cabbage, peas etc.)

Worcestershire sauce

salt and pepper

butter or margarine

shopping list

1 large onion

450 g/1 lb potatoes

1 crusty loaf

extra equipment

large frying pan (skillet)

fish slice

top tip!

If you don't have leftover cooked meat, a drained can of tuna fish or sliced hot dog sausages work equally well.

1   Peel and chop the onion.   ➡

2   Peel and dice the potatoes.   ➡

3   Cut the cooked meat into small pieces and roughly chop up the cooked vegetables.

4   Melt a large knob of butter or margarine in a frying pan and fry (sauté) the onion and potato over a medium heat for 10 minutes, stirring occasionally.

5   Turn on the oven at the lowest setting and put plates in to warm.

6   Add the meat and cooked vegetables, the baked beans and 1 tbsp Worcestershire sauce to the frying pan. Stir well and sprinkle with salt and pepper. Continue cooking and stirring for 5 minutes until piping hot.

7   Spoon the mixture on to the warm plates and serve with crusty bread.

➡   STEP 1. SEE PAGE 9

➡   STEP 2. SEE PAGE 10

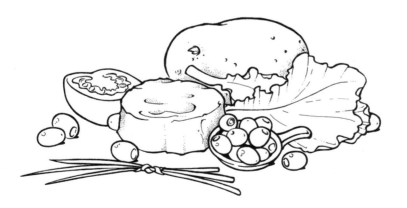

american red flannel hash
with crisp salad

SERVES 4

storecupboard ingredients

350 g/12 oz/1 large can of corned beef

sunflower oil

salt and pepper

milk

shopping list

2 rashers (slices) of rindless streaky bacon

2 large potatoes

1 onion

4 small cooked beetroot (red beets)

fresh parsley

curly endive (frisée lettuce)

2 large or 4 small tomatoes

extra equipment

grater

large frying pan (skillet)

fish slice

scissors

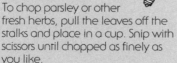

top tip!

To chop parsley or other fresh herbs, pull the leaves off the stalks and place in a cup. Snip with scissors until chopped as finely as you like.

1   Peel and dice the potatoes. Dice the beetroot in the same way. ➡

2   Peel and finely chop the onion. ➡

3   Cut the bacon into small pieces. Open the can of corned beef and mash the meat.

4   Chop a small handful of parsley (see Top Tip).

5   Heat about 3 tbsp oil in a large frying pan. Add the potatoes and onion and fry (sauté) over a fairly high heat for about 5 minutes, stirring occasionally, until almost cooked.

6   Add the bacon and cook for a further 1 minute.

7   Add the corned beef, beetroot, parsley and 2 tbsp milk and season with salt and pepper. Stir well, then press down with a fish slice to flatten. Cook over a high heat for 10 minutes until crisp and brown underneath.

8   Meanwhile, turn on the oven at the lowest setting and put a large serving platter and plates in to warm. Break up as much of the curly endive as you like into sprigs, wash and pat dry on kitchen paper (paper towels). Slice the tomatoes.

9   Put the large, warmed platter over the hash, then turn it over on to the platter, browned side up. Cut into wedges and serve with the curly endive and sliced tomatoes.

➡ STEP 1. SEE PAGE 10

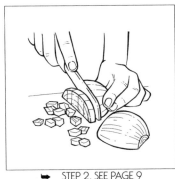

➡ STEP 2. SEE PAGE 9

nutty chicken stir-fry
with vegetables and noodles

SERVES 4

storecupboard ingredients

sunflower oil

1 chicken stock cube

cornflour (cornstarch)

walnut pieces

soy sauce

shopping list

1 packet of Chinese quick-cook egg noodles

225 g/8 oz chicken stir-fry meat

400 g/14 oz/1 large can of beansprouts

2 leeks

2 carrots

extra equipment

medium saucepan

colander

grater

large frying pan (skillet)

fish slice

kitchen scissors

small mixing bowl

measuring jug

top tip!
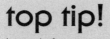

Instead of putting on the oven just to warm plates when you are boiling vegetables or cooking a one-pot meal, put the plates to heat on top of the pan with the lid over the top. When you are ready to serve, simply dry off any condensation with a tea towel (dish cloth).

1   Boil the kettle.

2   Put the chicken stock cube in a measuring jug and add 300 ml/
    ½ pt/1¼ cups boiling water. Stir until the cube dissolves.

3   Put two slabs of the noodles in a saucepan and cover with boiling
    water from the kettle. Put over a high heat until the water boils
    again. Cover with a lid, turn off the heat and leave for 5 minutes.

4   Put the colander in the sink. Pour in the noodles, then put the
    colander on top of the saucepan to finish draining.

5   Meanwhile, cut the root ends off the leeks and about 2.5 cm/1 in
    of the green tops. Peel off the tough outer layer. Cut the leeks into
    fairly thin round slices and rinse in a bowl of cold water. Swirl
    around a few times, then lift them out and dry on kitchen paper
    (paper towels).

6   Cut both ends off the carrots, peel with a knife or potato peeler
    and grate on the coarse side of the grater.

7   Heat 2 tbsp oil in the frying pan. Add the chicken, leeks and
    carrots and fry (sauté), stirring with the fish slice for 5 minutes.

8   Open the can of beansprouts and drain off the liquid. Add the
    beansprouts to the pan with a small handful of walnut pieces and
    the stock. Let the mixture bubble for 3 minutes.

9   Meanwhile, turn on the oven at the lowest setting and put plates
    in to warm. Mix 1 tbsp cornflour with 1 tbsp soy sauce in a small
    bowl until smooth. Stir into the chicken mixture and continue
    stirring until the mixture thickens.

10 Add the noodles and keep turning the mixture over carefully until
    everything is mixed and piping hot. Spoon on to the warm plates
    and serve.

spicy ginger stir-fry
with broccoli and beansprouts

SERVES 4

storecupboard ingredients

a good handful of leftover cooked chicken, turkey, pork, beef or peeled prawns (shrimp)
OR 425 g/ 15 oz/1 large can of beans or lentils, drained

frozen peas

sunflower oil

garlic purée (paste)

ground ginger

soy sauce

caster (superfine) sugar

dry sherry (optional)

shopping list
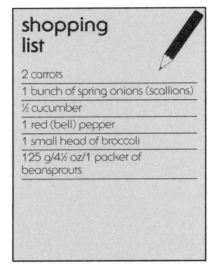

2 carrots

1 bunch of spring onions (scallions)

½ cucumber

1 red (bell) pepper

1 small head of broccoli

125 g/4½ oz/1 packet of beansprouts

extra equipment

large frying pan (skillet) or wok

fish slice or spatula

top tip!

Ring the changes by using any other vegetables of your choice. Make sure they are all cut into even-sized sticks, slices or florets. Always add the hardest ones (like root vegetables and celery) to the stir-fry first, then softer ones like courgettes (zucchini) and mushrooms after a minute or two.

1   Peel the carrots, cut off both ends, then cut each carrot into three pieces. Cut each piece into matchstick-sized strips.

2   Cut the half cucumber into strips the same size as the carrots.

3   Cut the root ends off the spring onions. Cut off the damaged part of the green tops. Pull off the outer, tough layer of each onion. Cut the onions into 5 cm/2 in lengths.

4   Cut the pepper in half, pull out the stalk, core and seeds, then cut the pepper into thin strips.

5   Cut the broccoli into tiny florets, discarding the thick, central stalk.

6   Cut any cooked meat you are using into small thin strips. Turn on the oven at the lowest setting and put plates in to warm.

7   Heat 2 tbsp oil in a frying pan or wok until it feels hot when you hold your hand about 5 cm/2 in above the surface. Add the carrots and onions and cook for 1 minute, stirring and turning in the oil. Add a good handful of peas, the cucumber, pepper and broccoli and stir-fry in the same way for a further 2 minutes. Add the beansprouts and stir-fry for 1 minute.

8   Add a good pinch of ginger, a small squeeze of garlic purée, a very good shake of soy sauce and a small splash of sherry. Stir-fry for 1 minute, then taste the liquid and sweeten with a sprinkling of sugar. Add your chosen meat, prawns or pulses and more soy sauce, if you like. Continue cooking and stirring for about 3 minutes until piping hot, then serve on the warm plates.

chunky cheeseburgers
and chips

SERVES 4

storecupboard ingredients

2 slices of stale bread

1 egg

dried onion granules

dried mixed herbs

salt and pepper

sunflower oil

tomato ketchup (catsup)

sliced dill pickles

Cheddar cheese
OR 4 slices of processed cheese

shopping list

350 g/12 oz lean minced (ground) beef

4 potatoes

4 soft white bread rolls

extra equipment

grater

large mixing bowl

2 frying pans (skillets)

1   Prepare the chips (fries). ➡

2   To make breadcrumbs, grate the bread slices on the coarse side of the grater or tear into pieces and chop until crumbly in a food processor.

3   Place in a large bowl with the minced meat. Add 1 tsp dried onion granules and 1 tsp dried mixed herbs. Sprinkle with salt and pepper and mix thoroughly with your hands.

4   Break the egg into a cup and stir briskly with a fork to mix the yolk and white together.

5   Pour into the meat mixture and mix well with your hands. Shape into four round burgers.

6   Cook the chips in a large frying pan. ➡

7   While they are cooking, heat 2 tbsp oil in another frying pan, add the burgers and fry (sauté) for 6 minutes, then carefully turn over with a fish slice and fry the other sides for a further 6 minutes until they are brown and cooked through. Drain on kitchen paper (paper towels).

8   Turn on the oven at the lowest setting and put plates in to warm. Drain the chips.

9   Preheat the grill (broiler). Split the rolls and place the bases on the grill (broiler) rack. Add a burger to each, top with a little ketchup, a couple of slices of dill pickle and a thin slice of Cheddar or a cheese slice. Put under the grill for 1–2 minutes until the cheese melts. Top with the lids of the rolls and transfer to the warm plates with the chips.

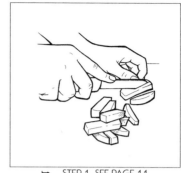
➡ STEP 1. SEE PAGE 11

➡ STEP 6. SEE PAGE 11

sweet and sour pork
with plain white rice

SERVES 4

storecupboard ingredients

240 g/8¾ oz/1 medium can of crushed pineapple

long-grain rice

sunflower oil

cornflour (cornstarch)

white wine vinegar

tomato ketchup (catsup)

soy sauce

shopping list

4 pork shoulder steaks

½ small cucumber

2 tomatoes

extra equipment

large saucepan

large frying pan (skillet)

colander

fish slice

1   Cook the rice. ➡

2   While the rice is cooking, prepare the rest of the dish. Cut the cucumber into small dice. Dice the tomatoes in the same way. ➡

3   Put 1 tbsp oil in a frying pan and heat until your hand feels hot when held 5 cm/2 in above it. Add the pork steaks and cook for a further 15 minutes until cooked through, turning once after 8 minutes.

4   Drain the rice. Turn the oven on at the lowest setting and put plates in to warm.

5   Lift the cooked pork out of the pan with a fish slice and place on a plate.

6   Empty the pineapple into the frying pan. Add 2 tbsp tomato ketchup and 1 tbsp soy sauce. Stir in the cucumber and tomato.

7   Mix 2 tsp cornflour with 1 tbsp vinegar in a cup and stir into the pan until it has thickened. Return the meat to the pan, turn over in the sauce and cook for 2 minutes.

8   Spoon the rice on to the warmed plates, top with the pork and sauce and serve.

➡ STEP 1. SEE PAGE 14

➡ STEP 2. SEE PAGE 10

spanish tortilla
with sweet pepper salad

SERVES 4

storecupboard ingredients

6 eggs

milk

olive oil

salt and pepper

red wine vinegar

caster (superfine) sugar

dried oregano

shopping list

2 onions

450 g/1 lb potatoes

2 red (bell) peppers

1 green pepper

1 round lettuce

1 crusty loaf

extra equipment

medium mixing bowl

balloon whisk

small mixing bowl

medium frying pan (skillet)

fish slice

salad bowl

top tip!

You can use a food processor or a gadget called a mandolin to slice potatoes and other vegetables thinly if you find it tricky to cut them by hand.

1   Chop one onion and slice the other.   ➡   ➡

➡ STEP 1. SEE PAGE 9

2   Scrub the potatoes or peel, if liked, then cut them into thin slices.

3   Heat 2 tbsp olive oil in a medium frying pan over a moderate heat. Add the chopped onion and the potatoes and fry (sauté) for about 5 minutes, stirring, until the potatoes and onions are transparent. If they begin to turn brown, turn down the heat.

4   Break the eggs into a medium bowl. Whisk until they are blended. Whisk in 4 tbsp milk and some salt and pepper. Rinse the whisk.

5   Pour the egg mixture into the pan and allow to cook slowly over a gentle heat until the egg is beginning to set. Lift the mixture gently at the sides with a fish slice as it sets to allow the runny egg to flow into the pan. When the mixture is almost set, cover the pan with a saucepan lid or foil and continue to cook until it has set completely.

➡ STEP 1. SEE PAGE 9

6   Meanwhile, put plates and a serving platter to warm in the oven at the lowest setting. Cut the peppers into halves lengthways and pull out the cores, stalk and seeds. Place on a board and cut into thin strips.

7   Wash the lettuce, pat dry on kitchen paper (paper towels) and tear into shreds. Place in the salad bowl and scatter the pepper strips over. Separate the sliced onion into rings and scatter over.

8   Put 3 tbsp olive oil in a small bowl with 1 tbsp red wine vinegar, a sprinkling of salt and pepper, 1 tsp caster sugar and ½ tsp dried oregano. Whisk with the rinsed balloon whisk until blended. Pour slowly all over the salad but don't toss it.

9   When the tortilla is completely set, loosen the base with the fish slice. Hold a serving platter over the frying pan, then invert so the brown side of the tortilla is uppermost on the platter.

10 Serve, cut into wedges, with the salad and crusty bread.

traditional british fish and chips
with peas and tartare sauce

SERVES 4

storecupboard ingredients

1 egg

frozen peas

plain (all-purpose) flour

sunflower oil

salt and pepper

tartare sauce or tomato ketchup (catsup)

shopping list
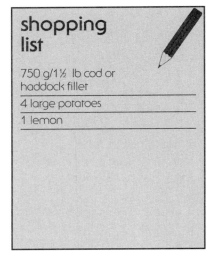

750 g/1½ lb cod or haddock fillet

4 large potatoes

1 lemon

extra equipment

large plate

measuring jug

mixing bowl

egg cup

saucer

small bowl

balloon whisk or electric hand beater

2 large frying pans (skillets)

medium saucepan

colander

top tip!
To store egg yolks, put them in a small container, cover with cold water and then a lid; they will keep in the fridge for up to three days. When required, drain off the water and beat. Use to glaze the tops of pies or brush over meat or fish before coating in breadcrumbs or stuffing mix.

1   Prepare the chips but do not cook them yet. ➡

2   Cut the fish into four equal pieces. Pull out any visible bones and lay the fish on a plate. Mix 2 tbsp plain flour with a little salt and pepper. Use to coat the fish thoroughly on both sides.

3   Measure 75 g/3 oz/¾ cup plain flour and put in the mixing bowl. Add a pinch of salt and 1 tbsp oil.

4   Separate the egg. ➡

5   Whisk the egg white with the balloon whisk or electric beater until fluffy and stiff. You should be able to turn the bowl upside down without the white falling out.

6   Measure 120 ml/4 fl oz/½ cup warm (not hot) water from the kettle. Gradually whisk into the flour mixture to make a smooth and thick batter. Spoon the egg white on top of the batter and gently stir into it with a metal spoon.

7   Heat 2.5 cm/1 in of oil in one frying pan for the chips. ➡ Heat a second frying pan with 1 cm/½ in oil for the fish. When hot, slide the chips into the deeper oil. Dip the pieces of fish, one at a time, into the batter until coated and put in the shallower hot oil. Cook for about 4 minutes on each side until golden brown and crispy.

8   While the fish and chips are cooking, turn on the oven at the lowest setting and put plates in to warm.

9   Boil 1 cm/½ in water in a saucepan. Add one handful of frozen peas per person and a pinch of salt. Cover with a lid and boil rapidly for 5 minutes. Drain in a colander in the sink.

10   When the fish and chips are brown all over, lift them out of their pans, and drain on plenty of kitchen paper (paper towels).

11   Transfer the fish, chips and peas on to the warm plates. Cut the lemon into four wedges and put one on each plate to garnish. Serve with tartare sauce or tomato ketchup.

➡ STEPS 1 AND 7. SEE PAGE 11

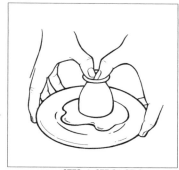

➡ STEP 4. SEE PAGE 8

trout with almonds
with baby new potatoes and mangetout

SERVES 4

storecupboard ingredients

butter or margarine

plain (all-purpose) flour

sunflower oil

salt and pepper

flaked (slivered) almonds

shopping list

4 rainbow trout, cleaned

fresh parsley

450 g/1 lb baby new potatoes

175 g/6 oz mangetout (snow peas)

extra equipment

large saucepan

colander

large frying pan (skillet)

fish slice

scissors

top tip!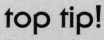

You can turn this recipe into another classic, Truite à la Meunière, by simply omitting the almonds and adding a squeeze of lemon juice.

1   Prepare the baby new potatoes and boil them over a moderate heat. ➡

2   Cut the stalks off the mangetout and place in a colander. Stand the colander over the pan of simmering potatoes, cover with a saucepan lid and cook for about 6 minutes until they are cooked to your liking, then remove from the pan.

3   While the vegetables are cooking, rinse the fish inside and out with cold running water, then pat dry with kitchen paper (paper towels). Sprinkle on both sides with flour and a little salt and pepper.

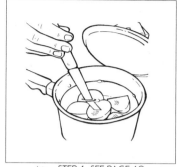

➡   STEP 1. SEE PAGE 10

4   Put a good knob of butter or margarine in a frying pan and about 2 tbsp sunflower oil. Heat over a moderate heat until sizzling. Add the fish and cook for 6 minutes.

5   Meanwhile, chop a small handful of parsley (see Top Tip page 20). Turn on the oven at the lowest setting and put plates in to warm.

6   Turn the fish over with a fish slice and a fork to guide them, scatter a small handful of flaked almonds over and fry (sauté) for a further 6 minutes until cooked through. Drain the potatoes.

7   Carefully lift the fish on to the warm plates. Pour any buttery juices over and sprinkle with the parsley. Serve with the new potatoes and mangetout.

flashy piquant steaks
with sauté potatoes and broccoli

SERVES 4

storecupboard ingredients

butter

lemon juice

Worcestershire sauce

salt

sunflower or olive oil

shopping list

4 thin frying steaks

1 small onion

4 potatoes

fresh parsley

1 medium head of broccoli

extra equipment

2 frying pans (skillets)

fish slice

medium saucepan

colander

shallow dish

1   Lay the steaks in a shallow dish and sprinkle all over with lemon juice. Leave to stand while preparing the potatoes.

2   Dice the potatoes. ➡

3   Finely chop the onion. ➡

4   Chop the parsley (see Top Tip page 20).

➡   STEP 2. SEE PAGE 10

5   Heat 5 mm/¼ in sunflower or olive oil in a frying pan. Add the diced potatoes and fry (sauté) until golden brown, turning over occasionally with the fish slice.

6   While the potatoes are cooking, turn on the oven at the lowest setting and put in plates and a shallow dish for the sauté potatoes to warm. Put a saucepan containing 2.5 cm/1 in water and a good pinch of salt on the hob over a high heat.

7   Melt a knob of butter in the other frying pan over a fairly high heat. Add the steaks and fry for 3 minutes on each side until browned and cooked through. Lift out of the pan and keep warm in the oven.

➡   STEP 3. SEE PAGE 9

8   While the steaks are cooking, cut the broccoli into separate little florets. Rinse with cold water. Add to the pan of boiling water, cover with a lid and cook for about 4 minutes until just tender. Drain in the colander in the sink.

9   Lift the sauté potatoes out of the pan with a fish slice and drain on kitchen paper (paper towels) in the warmed serving dish, slide off the kitchen paper and keep warm in the oven.

10 Add the chopped onion to the frying pan the steaks were in and fry for 1 minute. Add about 3 tbsp Worcestershire sauce and the parsley. Wait until it bubbles rapidly.

11 Put a steak on each of the warmed plates. Spoon the sauce over, add the sauté potatoes and broccoli and serve.

herb-coated turkey escalopes
with mashed potatoes and green beans

SERVES 4

storecupboard ingredients

85 g/3½ oz/1 packet of parsley, thyme and lemon stuffing mix

sunflower oil

salt and pepper

1 egg

butter or margarine

milk

shopping list

4 turkey breast steaks

750 g/1½ lb potatoes

225 g/8 oz French (green) beans

1 lemon

extra equipment

2 shallow dishes

rolling pin or meat mallet

large saucepan

colander

large frying pan (skillet)

fish slice

potato masher

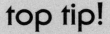
top tip!
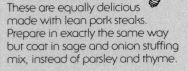
These are equally delicious made with lean pork steaks. Prepare in exactly the same way but coat in sage and onion stuffing mix, instead of parsley and thyme.

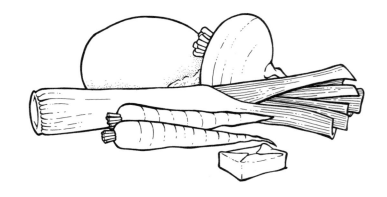

1   Prepare the potatoes and put them on to boil.   ➡

➡   STEP 1. SEE PAGE 10

2   Cut all the ends off the beans, place in a colander over the saucepan of potatoes, cover with the saucepan lid and steam over the potatoes.

3   Put the turkey breast steaks one at a time between sheets of clingfilm (plastic wrap) or in a plastic bag and beat with a rolling pin or meat mallet until flattened out.

4   Empty the stuffing mix into a shallow dish. Break the egg into another and stir well with a fork to mix thoroughly.

5   Dip the turkey steaks in the egg to cover both sides, letting the excess drain off back into the dish. Then dip in the stuffing until both sides are completely coated, again shaking any excess back into the dish.

6   Turn on the oven at the lowest setting and put in the plates and two serving dishes to warm.

7   Heat enough oil to cover the base of a frying pan. When it feels hot when you hold your hand about 5 cm/2 in above the surface, add the turkey escalopes and fry (sauté) for about 3–4 minutes until golden brown underneath. Carefully turn them over with a fish slice and a fork and cook the other sides. Drain on kitchen paper (paper towels) and place in the oven to keep warm.

8   While the turkey steaks are cooking, check the beans and potatoes. When they are cooked, transfer the beans to a serving dish and keep warm. Put the colander in the sink and tip in the potatoes to drain. Return the potatoes to the saucepan and add a good knob of butter or margarine and a splash of milk. Mash with a potato masher, adding a little more milk, if liked. Season with salt and pepper. Spoon into a serving dish and keep warm.

9   Cut the lemon into wedges. Transfer the turkey escalopes to the warm plates and garnish with lemon wedges. Serve with the mashed potatoes and beans.

french fried chicken
with green bean salad

SERVES 4

storecupboard ingredients

butter or margarine

olive oil

garlic purée (paste)

1 chicken stock cube

salt and pepper

red wine vinegar

shopping list

4 chicken portions

450 g/1 lb small waxy potatoes

100 g/4 oz button mushrooms

225 g/8 oz French (green) beans

1 small onion

fresh parsley

extra equipment

2 large frying pans (skillets)

small saucepan

colander

shallow serving dish

scissors

large serving platter

measuring jug

top tip!
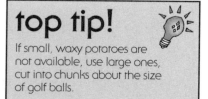

If small, waxy potatoes are not available, use large ones, cut into chunks about the size of golf balls.

1 Wash and dry the potatoes on kitchen paper (paper towels) but do not peel them. Heat a knob of butter and a little olive oil in a frying pan. Add the potatoes and fry (sauté), stirring occasionally, over a moderate heat, for about 10 minutes until browned all over.

2 At the same time, melt a knob of butter and a little oil in another frying pan. Fry the chicken portions on all sides over a fairly high heat until browned.

3 Wipe the mushrooms and cut into quarters if large. Add to the chicken with the potato pieces. Sprinkle with salt and pepper. Cover tightly with a lid or foil, turn down the heat and cook gently for 40 minutes until the chicken and potatoes are tender.

4 Meanwhile, cut the ends off the beans. Heat about 2.5 cm/1 in water in a saucepan with a pinch of salt. Add the beans, cover and boil for 4 minutes until almost tender but still slightly crunchy. Drain in a colander in the sink, rinse thoroughly with cold water, drain again and put in a shallow serving dish.

5 Finely chop the onion. Scatter over the beans. Trickle a little olive oil and vinegar over the surface and sprinkle with salt and pepper. Cover in clingfilm (plastic wrap) and chill until ready to serve. ➡

6 Finely chop a handful of parsley (see Top Tip page 20).

7 Turn on the oven at the lowest setting and put in plates and a large serving platter to warm.

8 Dot the chicken with tiny blobs of garlic purée. Sprinkle with half the parsley, re-cover and cook for a further 5 minutes.

9 Transfer the chicken, potatoes and mushrooms to the serving platter and keep warm. Crumble the stock cube into the juices left in the pan and add about 150 ml/¼ pt/⅔ cup water. Bring to the boil, stirring all the time and boil rapidly for 1 minute. Spoon over the chicken, sprinkle with the remaining parsley and serve hot with the green bean salad.

➡ STEP 5. SEE PAGE 9

7 grills

Grilling (broiling) is an excellent way of quick-cooking fish, poultry and tender cuts of meat. For best results, always preheat the grill (broiler) on high until it is glowing red before you start to cook.

sausage and mash
with onion and carrot gravy

SERVES 4

storecupboard ingredients

milk

butter or margarine

salt and pepper

plain (all-purpose) flour

1 beef or chicken stock cube

mustard

shopping list

450–750 g/1–1½ lb large pork sausages

900 g/2 lb potatoes

2 large onions

2 large carrots

extra equipment

measuring jug

grater

large saucepan

medium saucepan

small saucepan

scissors

colander

potato masher

1   Boil a kettle of water. Dissolve the stock cube in 450 ml/¾ pt/ 2 cups boiling water in a measuring jug.

2   Peel and boil the potatoes.   ➡

3   While the potatoes are cooking, slice the onions.   ➡   Peel and grate the carrots on the coarse side of a grater.

4   Put the onions and carrots in a small saucepan and add a small knob of butter or margarine. Cook over a high heat, stirring, for 2 minutes.

5   Pour in the stock, cover with a lid and cook for 5 minutes.

6   Turn on the grill (broiler) to preheat. Snip between the sausages with scissors, to separate, and place on the rack. Grill (broil) for about 10 minutes, until brown all over, giving the sausages a quarter turn every few minutes. Put four plates to warm in the oven at the lowest setting.

7   Put 3 tbsp flour in a measuring jug. Add 5 tbsp cold water and stir until the mixture is smooth. Add to the stock, onion and carrots, stirring all the time until thickened. Turn the heat down really low. Taste and season with salt and pepper.

8   Put the colander in the sink and pour the potatoes into it. Shake the colander to drain off all the water, then tip the potatoes back in the pan.

9   Add a knob of butter or margarine and mash thoroughly with a potato masher. Add a dash of milk and mash again. Add more milk if you like your mashed potato softer.

10   Pile the potato on to the warm plates. Top with the sausages and spoon some onion and carrot gravy over. Serve with mustard.

➡   STEP 2. SEE PAGE 10

➡   STEP 3. SEE PAGE 9

kofta kebabs
with cucumber rice and spicy tomato sauce

SERVES 4

storecupboard ingredients

3 slices of stale bread

1 egg

long-grain rice

sunflower oil

caster (superfine) sugar

tomato ketchup (catsup)

Tabasco sauce

Worcestershire sauce

mixed (apple-pie) spice

garlic purée (paste)

tomato purée

dried mint

salt and pepper

shopping list

450 g/1 lb minced (ground) beef or lamb

fresh parsley

1 onion

1 lemon

½ cucumber

extra equipment

food processor or grater

scissors

mixing bowl

4 metal kebab skewers

large saucepan

medium saucepan

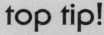

top tip!

A bunch of fresh parsley will keep fresh for a week or two if kept in a jug of water on the window sill. Change the water frequently. Alternatively, store in the vegetable chiller in the fridge.

1   Break the slices of bread into pieces. Drop into a food processor with the machine running to make breadcrumbs. Alternatively, rub the bread on the coarse side of a grater to make the crumbs.

2   Chop a small handful of parsley (see Top Tip page 20).

3   Put the crumbs in a bowl with the parsley, minced meat, ½ tsp mixed spice and a small squeeze of garlic purée and mix together well.

4   Break the egg into a cup and beat lightly with a fork until blended. Add to the meat mixture and mix well with your hands.

5   With wet hands, take handfuls of the mixture and shape in sausages around kebab skewers. Lay on foil on the grill (broiler) rack.

6   Dice the cucumber. ➡

7   Cook the rice, adding the cucumber and 1 tsp dried mint after 10 minutes. ➡

8   Chop the onion. ➡

9   Heat 2 tbsp oil in a medium saucepan. Add the onion and cook for 2 minutes, stirring occasionally. Add 3 tbsp caster sugar, 3 tbsp tomato ketchup, 1 tbsp tomato purée and a few drops each of Tabasco and Worcestershire sauce. Stir well and season with salt and pepper. Cook over a moderate heat, stirring until boiling, then leave it to bubble for 3 minutes. Turn off the heat.

10 Turn on the grill (broiler) to preheat, turn on the oven at the lowest setting and put in plates to warm.

11 Grill (broil) the kebabs under the hot grill for 6 minutes on each side until cooked through and browned.

12 Spoon the rice on to the warm plates, top with the kebabs and spoon the sauce over.

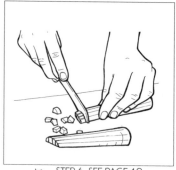
➡ STEP 6. SEE PAGE 10

➡ STEP 7. SEE PAGE 14

➡ STEP 8. SEE PAGE 9

greek-style lamb kebabs
with pitta bread and village salad

SERVES 4

storecupboard ingredients

olive oil

salt and pepper

dried oregano

garlic purée (paste)

red wine vinegar

shopping list

350 g/12 oz lamb neck fillets

2 courgettes (zucchini)

1 iceburg lettuce

2 tomatoes

1 cucumber

1 onion

1 packet of pitta breads

100 g/4 oz Feta cheese

1 jar of black olives

extra equipment

large, shallow dish

balloon whisk

4 metal kebab skewers

pastry brush

salad bowl

top tip!

These kebabs work just as well with pork fillet or chicken breasts instead of the lamb fillets.

1 Cut the lamb into bite-sized cubes, cutting off any fat or gristle.

2 Pour enough oil into a shallow dish to coat the base. Add a good splash of vinegar, a good sprinkling of dried oregano, a small squeeze of garlic purée and a little salt and pepper. Mix with a balloon whisk until thoroughly blended.

3 Add the meat to the dish and turn over using your fingers until every piece is coated and glistening. Cover with foil and leave to marinate in the fridge for at least 2 hours – the longer, the better.

4 Prepare your village salad. First, make a mixed salad, using the lettuce, tomatoes, onion and cucumber. ➡

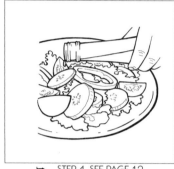

➡ STEP 4. SEE PAGE 12

5 Cut the Feta cheese into chunks or roughly crumble and sprinkle over the surface of the mixed salad. Dot with a few olives. Trickle some olive oil over the surface, then sprinkle with a little vinegar (quantities are not vital, but use less vinegar than oil), pepper (preferably freshly ground) and a pinch of dried oregano. Leave to stand while cooking the kebabs.

6 Turn on the grill (broiler) to preheat. Cut the ends off the courgettes, then cut them into chunks about 1 cm/½ in long. Thread the meat on the skewers, interspersed with pieces of courgette.

7 Lay the kebabs on the grill rack and brush with any marinade left in the dish. Grill for 10 minutes, turning once or twice and brushing with the marinade from time to time.

8 While the kebabs are cooking, turn on the oven at the lowest setting. Wrap four pitta breads in foil and pop them in to warm briefly. When the kebabs are cooked, make a slit the length of one edge of each pitta bread and gently open to form a pocket. Slide a kebab off its skewer and put into the pitta pocket. Repeat with the remaining kebabs and pittas. You can eat these in your fingers, but don't forget to put out forks for the village salad!

grilled steaks
with mushrooms and french fries

SERVES 4

storecupboard ingredients

sunflower oil

salt and pepper

Dijon or English mustard

butter or margarine

frozen peas

shopping list

4 lean rump or sirloin steaks, about 175 g/6 oz each

4 large potatoes

225 g/8 oz button mushrooms

2 tomatoes

extra equipment

large frying pan (skillet)

large saucepan

small saucepan

fish slice or draining spoon

1   Make the chips (fries). ➡

2   While they are cooking, wipe the mushrooms. Put enough water in a medium saucepan to cover the base, add the mushrooms, a good knob of butter or margarine and some salt and pepper. Cover with a lid and cook over a moderate heat while preparing the rest of the meal. When steam starts to come from the saucepan, turn the heat down low.

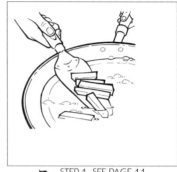

➡ STEP 1. SEE PAGE 11

3   Turn on the grill (broiler) to preheat. Put 1 cm/½ in water in a small saucepan with a pinch of salt and place over a moderate heat to come to the boil. Meanwhile, smear a little oil over the steaks, season with pepper and place on the grill rack. Grill (broil) until brown and cooked to your liking; this will take at least 4 minutes each side for medium rare or about 6 minutes a side for well-done (depending on the thickness of the steak).

4   When the steaks are cooking, turn on the oven at the lowest setting and put in plates and a shallow dish to warm. Add a small handful of peas per person to the boiling water in the small saucepan and cook for 5 minutes.

5   The chips should now be cooked. Line the warmed serving dish with a double thickness of kitchen paper (paper towels). Remove the chips from the pan with a fish slice or draining spoon and pile in the dish. Remove the paper and place the chips in the oven to keep warm.

6   Cut the tomatoes into halves. Drain the peas in a colander in the sink. Transfer the steaks to the warm plates. Add the mushrooms, chips and peas and garnish each plate with half a tomato. Serve with Dijon or English mustard.

steak chasseur
with sauté potatoes and mixed salad

SERVES 4

storecupboard ingredients

sunflower oil

red wine

1 beef stock cube

tomato purée (paste)

garlic purée

caster (superfine) sugar

salt and pepper

dried mixed herbs

olive oil

wine vinegar

shopping list

4 fillet steaks, about 150 g/ 5 oz each

4 fairly large potatoes

125 g/4½ oz packet of mixed salad leaves

2 tomatoes

1 cucumber

1 onion

fresh parsley

extra equipment

large frying pan (skillet)

measuring jug

small saucepan

salad bowl

top tip!

You can substitute chicken pieces for the steaks, but remember to use a chicken stock cube instead of beef and make sure the chicken is cooked right through..

1   Dice the potatoes.

2   Heat about 5 mm/¼ in oil in a large frying pan.

3   While the oil is heating, turn on the grill (broiler) to preheat. Turn on the oven at the lowest setting and put in plates and a shallow serving dish to warm. Put the steaks on the grill rack. Smear with a little sunflower oil and season with pepper. Grill for 8–12 minutes, turning once, until cooked to your liking.

4   While the steaks are cooking, slide the potatoes into the hot oil and fry (sauté) until golden brown all over, turning occasionally with a fish slice.

5   Put 150 ml/¼ pt/⅔ cup water and the same amount of red wine in a saucepan with the stock cube. Bring to the boil and stir until the cube has dissolved.

6   Stir a large squeeze of tomato purée and a very small squeeze of garlic purée into the wine and stock. Stir until blended and the mixture is bubbling. Add about 2 tsp caster sugar, a sprinkling of dried mixed herbs and salt and pepper to taste. Let the sauce bubble rapidly until it thickens and has reduced in quantity.

7   Make a mixed salad and French dressing.

8   When the potatoes are cooked, put a double thickness of kitchen paper (paper towels) in the warmed serving dish. Remove the potatoes with a fish slice or draining spoon and drain on the paper. Remove the paper and put the potatoes in the oven to keep warm.

9   Transfer the cooked steaks to the warmed plates. Spoon the sauce over, garnish each with a sprig of parsley and add the sauté potatoes. Serve the salad separately.

➥ STEP 1. SEE PAGE 10

➥ STEP 7. SEE PAGE 12

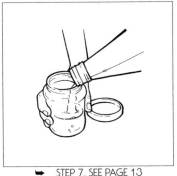

➥ STEP 7. SEE PAGE 13

gammon steaks
with fresh kiwi slices, golden scallops and peas

SERVES 4

storecupboard ingredients

sunflower oil

frozen peas

shopping list

4 fairly large potatoes

4 gammon steaks

2 kiwi fruit

2 tomatoes

extra equipment

large frying pan (skillet)

fish slice

scissors

small saucepan

1   Prepare and cook the golden scallops like chips (fries), but cut the potatoes into 5 mm/¼ in thick slices and cook them whole. ➡

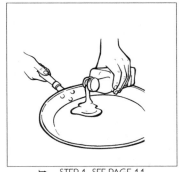

➡   STEP 1. SEE PAGE 11

2   Meanwhile, turn on the grill (broiler) to preheat. Turn on the oven at the lowest setting and put in plates and a serving dish for the potatoes to warm. Put about 1 cm/½ in water in a small saucepan with a pinch of salt and put on to heat.

3   Cut both ends off the kiwi fruit and peel off the skin. Cut each fruit into four thick slices.

4   Snip all round the edges of the gammon steaks with scissors to prevent the edges from curling up while they cook. Place on the grill rack. Grill (broil) for 4 minutes.

5   Put a handful of peas per person in the small saucepan of water, which should now be boiling, cover with a lid and boil for 5 minutes. Check the potatoes, and if browned all over, put a double thickness of kitchen paper (paper towels) in the warmed serving dish. Lift the potatoes out of the oil with a fish slice and drain on the paper. Remove the paper, then put the potatoes in the oven to keep warm. If the potatoes are not ready, leave them until you have turned the gammon over (see step 6).

6   Cut the tomatoes into halves. Turn the gammon steaks over and put the tomato halves on the grill rack too. Put two slices of kiwi fruit on top of each gammon steak. Return to the grill and cook for about 3 minutes until browned and cooked through.

7   Drain the peas into a colander in the sink.

8   Transfer the gammon, topped with kiwi fruit, and the tomato halves to the warm plates. Add the golden scallops and peas and serve straight away.

grilled pork chops
with peaches, new potatoes and green beans

SERVES 4

storecupboard ingredients

410g/14½ oz/1 large can of peach halves

salt and pepper

dried sage

2 glacé (candied) cherries

shopping list

4 pork chops

450 g/1 lb new potatoes

175 g/6 oz French (green) beans

1 bunch of watercress

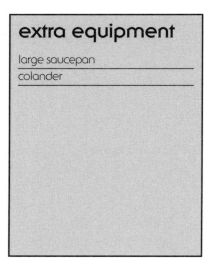

extra equipment

large saucepan

colander

top tip!

For a change, try using lamb chops instead of pork and sprinkling them with dried rosemary instead of sage.

1   Prepare the new potatoes and put them on to boil.   ➡

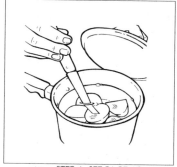

➡ STEP 1. SEE PAGE 10

2   As soon as you have put them on, cut the tops and tails off the French beans and place in a colander. Put the colander over the pan of boiling potatoes, cover with the saucepan lid and leave them to steam.

3   Turn on the grill (broiler) to preheat. Put the pork chops on the grill rack. Sprinkle with pepper and a fine dusting of dried sage. Turn over and repeat on the other sides. Grill (broil) for 8 minutes until golden brown. Turn the chops over and grill for another 8 minutes.

4   Meanwhile, lift the peach halves out of their juice and drain on kitchen paper (paper towels). Turn on the oven at the lowest setting and put in plates and two serving dishes to warm. When the chops have been cooking for 5 minutes on the second side, add the peach halves to the grill rack and put a halved glacé cherry in the centre of each. Grill for a further 3 minutes.

5   Cut the ends of the feathery stalks off the watercress, rinse the sprigs of leaves and dry on kitchen paper. Lift the colander off the top of the potatoes and check that the beans are cooked. Turn them into a warmed serving dish and keep warm. Drain the potatoes into the colander, then transfer to the other warmed serving dish.

6   Put the chops on the warmed plates with the grilled peach halves. Garnish with sprigs of watercress and serve with the new potatoes and beans.

mighty mixed grill
with french-style peas

SERVES 4

storecupboard ingredients

butter

frozen peas

dried mint

plain potato crisps (chips)

English mustard

shopping list

4 lamb cutlets

4 lambs' kidneys

4 pork sausages

4 rashers (slices) of back bacon

1 onion

1 small lettuce

2 tomatoes

1 bunch of watercress

extra equipment

1 medium saucepan

scissors

small saucepan

pastry brush

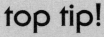

top tip!

You can vary the ingredients of a mixed grill as much as you like; try using small pork chops or pieces of rump or fillet steak instead of lamb cutlets.

1   Peel and chop the onion.   ➡

2   Rinse the lettuce and cut into fairly thin shreds.

3   Melt a knob of butter in a saucepan, add the onion and cook over a fairly gentle heat, stirring with a wooden spoon until the onion is soft but not brown.

4   Add a good handful of peas per person, the lettuce, a good sprinkling of mint and some salt and pepper. Add 2 tbsp water. Cover with a lid, keep the heat low and leave to cook very gently while you prepare the mixed grill.

5   Trim any fat from the lamb cutlets. Cut the kidneys into halves with scissors and snip out the white central cores. Arrange the kidneys on a grill (broiler) rack with the sausages, but don't start to cook them yet.

6   Turn on the grill to preheat. Melt a good knob of butter in a small saucepan and brush over the lamb and kidneys. Put under the grill and cook for 3 minutes. Put a shallow ovenproof serving dish to warm under the grill if there is room. If not, put it in the oven at the lowest setting.

7   Stir the peas. Put plates to warm over the saucepan, with the lid on top, or in the oven. Turn the meat over. Cut the tomatoes into halves and add to the grill with the bacon. Brush all the ingredients with butter and continue cooking for a further 4 minutes until everything is cooked through.

8   Trim the stalks off the watercress. Rinse the sprigs of leaves and pat dry on kitchen paper (paper towels).

9   Spoon the peas into the warmed serving dish. Transfer the mixed grill to the warm plates, garnish with watercress and potato crisps and serve with the peas.

➡ STEP 1. SEE PAGE 9

oregano lemon chicken
on a vegetable platter

SERVES 4

storecupboard ingredients

sunflower oil

salt and pepper

dried oregano

lemon juice

caster (superfine) sugar

frozen peas

shopping list

4 chicken portions

2 large potatoes

2 large carrots

2 turnips

extra equipment

large saucepan

small bowl

balloon whisk

pastry brush

1   Peel and cut all the vegetables into small dice.   ➡

2   Place in a large saucepan, cover with cold water and sprinkle with salt. Put over a high heat, cover with a lid and wait until it boils rapidly. Reduce the heat and let it bubble gently for about 8 minutes.

3   While the vegetables are cooking, turn on the grill (broiler) to preheat. Rub the chicken all over with a little oil and sprinkle with salt and pepper. Place on the grill rack, skin-side down and cook for 7 minutes. Put the plates to warm under the grill if there is room, or in the oven at the lowest setting.

4   While the chicken is cooking, add two handfuls of frozen peas to the vegetables and continue cooking until all the vegetables are just tender.

5   Turn the chicken over and cook for a further 5 minutes. Put 3 tbsp oil in a small bowl. Add 3 tbsp lemon juice, 2 tsp dried oregano and 1 tsp caster sugar. Whisk together well. Brush all over the chicken and return to the grill for a further 2 minutes. Brush again and cook for about 2 minutes more until crisp, brown and cooked right through.

6   While the chicken is finishing cooking, drain the vegetables into a colander in the sink.

7   Spoon the vegetables on to the warm plates and top with the chicken.

➡   STEP 1. SEE PAGE 10

grilled salmon fillets
with hollandaise sauce, new potatoes and salad

SERVES 4

storecupboard ingredients

butter

salt and pepper

good-quality mayonnaise

lemon juice

olive oil

wine vinegar

caster (superfine) sugar

shopping list

4 salmon tail fillets (about 175 g/6 oz) each

450 g/1 lb baby new potatoes

125 g/4½ oz packet of mixed salad leaves

1 cucumber

1 green (bell) pepper

1 onion

1 avocado

extra equipment

large saucepan

small bowl

small saucepan

balloon whisk

salad bowl

top tip!

You can make a green Hollandaise sauce to serve with salmon, other fish or grilled chicken breasts. Simply chop a handful of watercress or fresh herbs, (see Top Tip page 20) and add to the sauce.

1   Prepare and boil the potatoes.   ➡

2   Prepare a green salad and French dressing.   ➡   ➡

3   Cut the avocado in half, remove the stone (pit), then pull off the skin. If it is very ripe it should come away easily, if not, use a sharp knife to peel it. Cut the flesh into slices, put in a small bowl and sprinkle with lemon juice to prevent browning, then add to the salad.

➡   STEP 1. SEE PAGE 10

4   Arrange the salmon steaks on the grill (broiler) rack, dot with butter and season with pepper. Turn on the grill to preheat but don't put the fish under yet.

5   To make the Hollandaise sauce, melt 25 g/1 oz/2 tbsp butter in a small saucepan over a gentle heat. When the butter has melted, turn the heat down very low and whisk in 8 tbsp mayonnaise, using a balloon whisk. Continue to whisk until the mixture is smooth and glossy. Add a dash of lemon juice and whisk again. Turn off the heat but leave the pan on the cooker.

➡   STEP 2. SEE PAGE 12

6   Turn on the oven at the lowest setting and put in plates to warm.

7   Grill (broil) the fish steaks for 5–6 minutes until lightly golden and cooked through. Don't turn them over.

8   Carefully transfer the steaks to the warm plates, add a spoonful of the Hollandaise sauce to each and serve with the new potatoes and dressed green avocado salad.

➡   STEP 2. SEE PAGE 13

thai-style whiting
with fragrant rice

SERVES 4

storecupboard ingredients

frozen peas

Thai fragrant rice (or basmati rice)

salt and pepper

light brown sugar

ground ginger

chilli powder

shopping list

4 whiting fillers, about 150 g/5 oz each

1 lime

extra equipment

large saucepan

grater

citrus squeezer

1   Cook 175 g/6 oz/¾ cup rice, adding two good handfuls of peas halfway through cooking. ➡

➡   STEP 1. SEE PAGE 14

2   While the rice is cooking, put a sheet of foil on the grill (broiler) rack. Lay the fish on the foil. Grate the rind off the lime on the coarse side of a grater, then cut the lime in half and squeeze out the juice.

3   Sprinkle the fish fillets with a little salt and half the lime juice and leave to stand for 10 minutes.

4   Turn on the grill and put plates under to warm if there is room. If not, put in the oven at the lowest setting.
Sprinkle the fish with
2 tbsp brown sugar and grill (broil) for 5 minutes until the sugar is bubbling and caramelised.

5   Sprinkle a good pinch of ginger and chilli powder over the drained rice and gently stir in.

6   Pile on to the warm plates and top with a fish fillet. Sprinkle with the remaining lime juice and the lime rind.

8 one-pot meals

All these dishes are very quick and easy to prepare, and once everything is in the pot you can just leave them to cook. What's more, there is very little washing up! The top-of-the-stove meals can also be cooked in the oven at 160°F/325°C/gas mark 3 for the indicated time – longer, if you prefer.

traditional irish stew
with crusty bread

SERVES 4

storecupboard ingredients

salt and pepper

shopping list

750 g/1½ lb best end of neck of lamb cutlets

900 g/2 lb potatoes

2 large onions

2 large carrots

1 crusty loaf

extra equipment

large, flameproof casserole (Dutch oven)

kitchen scissors

draining spoon

1   Trim off all the skin and fat from the cutlets with kitchen scissors.

2   Peel the potatoes and carrots and cut into rounds about
     5 mm/¼ in thick.

3   Peel and slice the onions.   ➡

➡ STEP 3. SEE PAGE 9

4   Put half the cutlets in the base of the casserole dish. Sprinkle with
     a little salt and pepper.

5   Cover with half the onions, then half the carrots and add a little
     more salt and pepper. Add half the potatoes and another
     sprinkling of salt and pepper. Repeat these layers with the rest of
     the ingredients.

6   Pour in just enough water to come up to the top layer of potatoes,
     but don't cover them.

7   Put over a high heat until the water boils. Use a draining spoon to
     skim off any white scum from the surface. Cover with a lid, turn
     the heat down as low as possible and leave to cook for 2 hours
     until everything is really tender.

8   Turn on the grill (broiler) to preheat. Remove the lid and place the
     casserole dish under the grill for about 5 minutes until the
     potatoes are browning on top. Serve straight from the pot with
     crusty bread.

welsh pot warmer
with hot wholemeal rolls

SERVES 4

storecupboard ingredients

1 bouquet garni sachet

salt and pepper

1 chicken stock cube

dried parsley

shopping list

4 chicken portions

2 leeks

2 turnips

2 large carrots

450 g/1 lb small, waxy potatoes

4 wholemeal rolls

extra equipment

large saucepan

measuring jug

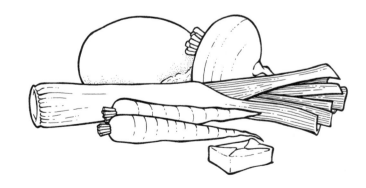

top tip!

This dish is also delicious made with 2 small breasts of lamb. Chop them into ribs and cut the excess fat off before cooking.

1   Pull as much skin as possible off the chicken portions and discard.

2   Cut the roots off the leeks, trim off the tops, pull off the damaged outer leaves, then cut into slices and place in a bowl of cold water to clean thoroughly.

3   Peel and cut the carrots and turnips into large chunks.   ➡

4   Rinse the potatoes.

5   Drain the leeks and place in a large saucepan with the chicken, carrots, turnips and potatoes. Add 900 ml/1½ pts/3 cups water and crumble in the stock cube. Sprinkle with salt and pepper and add the bouquet garni sachet and a little dried parsley.

6   Put over a high heat and wait until the water is bubbling fiercely. Turn down the heat until the liquid is only gently bubbling. Cover with a lid and let it cook for 1 hour. Put four large soup bowls to warm over the saucepan for the last 15 minutes of cooking time.

7   Transfer the chicken and vegetables to the soup bowls, discarding the bouquet garni sachet. Taste the cooking liquid and add more salt and pepper, if necessary. Pour into the bowls and serve with wholemeal rolls.

➡ STEP 3. SEE PAGE 10

hungarian goulash
with rye bread

SERVES 4

storecupboard ingredients

400 g/14 oz/1 large can of chopped tomatoes

sunflower oil

paprika

salt and pepper

tomato purée (paste)

garlic purée

caster (superfine) sugar

plain (all-purpose) flour

shopping list

550g/1¼ lb lean diced stewing steak

1 large onion

2 large carrots

3 large potatoes

1 small carton of soured (dairy sour) cream

caraway seeds (optional)

1 small rye loaf

extra equipment

large saucepan or flameproof casserole (Dutch oven)

top tip!

This dish is so versatile, it is equally delicious made with diced pork or lamb.

1   Trim off any fat or gristle from the meat, if necessary.

2   Peel and chop the onion. ➡

3   Peel and cut the carrots and potatoes into bite-sized chunky pieces. ➡

4   Heat 1 tbsp oil in a large saucepan or flameproof casserole. Add the meat and onion and cook over a high heat, stirring until the meat is browned all over and the onions are colouring slightly.

➡ STEP 2. SEE PAGE 9

5   Sprinkle in 1 tbsp paprika and stir well.

6   Add the contents of the can of tomatoes. Fill up the can with water and add that too. Stir in the carrots and potatoes, a good squeeze of tomato purée, a small squeeze of garlic purée and a pinch of sugar. Add a little salt and pepper and stir until well blended. Let the mixture come to the boil.

7   When bubbling, turn the heat right down, stir again, cover with a lid and cook gently for 2 hours, stirring occasionally. Towards the end of the cooking time, stand large soup bowls over the pan, under the lid, to warm, or place in the oven at the lowest setting.

➡ STEP 3. SEE PAGE 10

8   Mix 2 tbsp flour with 4 tbsp water in a cup until smooth. Stir into the goulash and cook, stirring, for 2 minutes until thickened. Taste and add more salt and pepper, if necessary.

9   Spoon into the warm soup bowls. Add a spoonful of soured cream to each and sprinkle with caraway seeds, if liked. Serve with hunks of rye bread.

garbanzos a la rustica
with crusty bread

SERVES 4

storecupboard ingredients

2 x 430 g/2 x 15½ oz/2 large cans of chick peas (garbanzos)

2 chicken stock cubes

olive oil

tomato purée (paste)

garlic purée

salt and pepper

ground cumin

dried mixed herbs

shopping list

225 g/8 oz belly pork slices

100 g/4 oz chorizo sausage (in one piece)

2 large onions

2 large potatoes

½ small green cabbage

1 crusty loaf

extra equipment

large saucepan

kitchen scissors

1   Cut the rind and any bones off the pork with scissors, then cut the meat into bite-sized cubes.

2   Cut the chorizo sausage into chunks.

3   Chop the onions. ➡

4   Peel and cut the potatoes into large chunks. ➡

5   Heat 2 tbsp olive oil in a saucepan over a high heat. Add the pork and onions and cook for 2 minutes, stirring all the time.

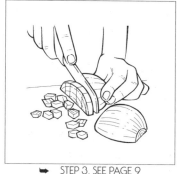

➡ STEP 3. SEE PAGE 9

6   Add the contents of the cans of chick peas, including the liquid, the sausage chunks, potatoes, crumbled stock cubes and 600 ml/ 1 pt/2½ cups water. Wait until the water boils, stirring occasionally, then add a good squeeze of tomato purée and a small squeeze of garlic purée.

7   Sprinkle about 1 tsp ground cumin and about ½ tsp dried mixed herbs over the surface with some salt and pepper, and stir. Part-cover with a lid, reduce the heat to low and let it cook gently for 1 hour.

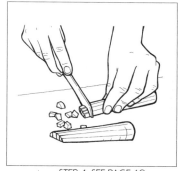

➡ STEP 4. SEE PAGE 10

8   Cut the central core out of the cabbage, then cut into thin slices so it separates into shreds. Add to the saucepan, stir again and let it continue cooking for 30 minutes.

9   A few minutes before the end of the cooking time, place large bowls on top of the pan, under the lid, to warm, or place in the oven at the lowest setting.

10 Spoon into the warm bowls and serve with crusty bread.

pot roast chicken
with winter vegetables

SERVES 4–6

storecupboard ingredients

1 chicken stock cube

1 bouquet garni sachet

1 bay leaf

salt and pepper

shopping list

1.6 kg/3½ lb oven-ready chicken

2 onions

2 carrots

1 parsnip

4 large potatoes

2 celery sticks

extra equipment

large casserole dish (Dutch oven)

1   Turn on the oven to 190°C/375°F/gas mark 5.

2   Boil a kettle of water.

3   Remove any giblets from inside the chicken. Wipe the chicken inside and out with kitchen paper (paper towels). Pull out any excess fat from just inside the body cavity and discard.

4   Chop the onions.   ➡

5   Chop the celery sticks into short lengths. Peel and cut the carrots, parsnip and potatoes into large dice.   ➡

6   Put half the vegetables in the casserole and sit the chicken on top. Add the bouquet garni and bay leaf. Pack the rest of the vegetables around the bird.

7   Measure 300 ml/½ pt/1¼ cups boiling water into a measuring jug and dissolve the stock cube in it. Pour over the chicken and sprinkle with a little salt and pepper.

8   Cover with a lid and cook in the oven for 1½ hours. At the end of the cooking time, put plates in to warm. Carefully lift the chicken out of the pot and cut it into pieces (it will probably fall apart). Discard the bouquet garni and the bay leaf. Serve the chicken with the vegetables and the juices.

➡   STEP 4. SEE PAGE 9

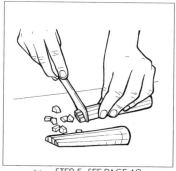

➡   STEP 5. SEE PAGE 10

fragrant fish pot
with crusty bread

SERVES 4

storecupboard ingredients

butter or margarine

400 g/14 oz/1 large can of chopped tomatoes

dried basil

salt and pepper

shopping list
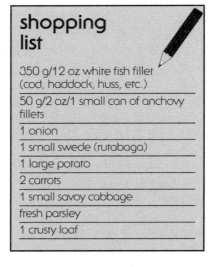

350 g/12 oz white fish fillet (cod, haddock, huss, etc.)

50 g/2 oz/1 small can of anchovy fillets

1 onion

1 small swede (rutabaga)

1 large potato

2 carrots

1 small savoy cabbage

fresh parsley

1 crusty loaf

extra equipment

large saucepan

scissors

soup ladle

top tip!

When skinning fish, dip your finger and thumb in salt before holding on to the skin – it will stop it slipping through your fingers.

1   Thinly slice the onion. ➡

2   Peel and dice the swede, potato and carrots. ➡

3   Cut out the thick central stalk from the cabbage, then cut the cabbage into thin slices and separate into shreds.

4   Using a sharp knife, make a cut between the skin and the flesh of the fish at one end, then, holding the skin firmly between your finger and thumb, cut and scrape the flesh away from the skin, gently pulling the skin as you go. (see Top Tip opposite). You may find that once you've created a flap you can pull the skin off. Cut the fish into large chunks.

5   Open the can of anchovies and pour off all the oil. Put the anchovies on the chopping board and cut them into small pieces.

6   Melt a large knob of butter or margarine in a large saucepan. Add all the prepared vegetables and cook, stirring occasionally with a wooden spoon, for 10 minutes over a low heat.

7   Add the contents of the can of tomatoes. Fill the can up with water and add to the pan. Stir in the anchovies. Turn up the heat until the mixture is boiling rapidly, then turn it down to moderate and let it bubble gently for 10 minutes, stirring once or twice.

8   Add the fish, together with about ½ tsp dried basil and some pepper. Put large soup bowls to warm over the saucepan and cover with a lid, or place in the oven at the lowest setting. Cook for a further 10 minutes until the vegetables and fish are tender. Remove the bowls, taste and add salt and pepper, if necessary.

9   Chop a few sprigs of parsley (see Top Tip page 20). Ladle the fish and vegetables into the warmed bowls, sprinkle with chopped parsley and serve with crusty bread.

➡ STEP 1. SEE PAGE 9

➡ STEP 2. SEE PAGE 10

winter beef pot
with horseradish dumplings

SERVES 4

storecupboard ingredients

1 beef stock cube

gravy block or browning

1 bay leaf

self-raising (self-rising) flour

shredded vegetable suet

salt and pepper

plain (all-purpose) flour

horseradish relish or sauce

shopping list

550 g/1¼ lb lean stewing steak

2 large onions

2 large carrots

1 small swede (rutabaga)

4 large potatoes

extra equipment

large saucepan

draining spoon

mixing bowl

1   Cut the meat into bite-sized pieces, discarding any fat or gristle. Place in the saucepan.

2   Roughly chop the onions.   ➡

3   Prepare and cut the carrots and swede into chunks.   ➡

➡   STEP 2. SEE PAGE 9

4   Put the prepared vegetables on top of the meat. Add just enough cold water to cover all the ingredients.

5   Put in the bay leaf, crumble in the stock cube and sprinkle lightly with salt and pepper. Put the pan over a high heat and wait until the water boils. Skim off any white scum from the surface, using a draining spoon.

6   Turn down the heat until the liquid is just gently bubbling, cover with a lid and leave it to cook gently for 2 hours.

7   Peel the potatoes and cut into large chunks. Measure 100 g/ 4 oz/1 cup self-raising flour into a mixing bowl. Add 3 tbsp vegetable suet, 2 tbsp horseradish relish or sauce and a good pinch of salt. Gradually stir in some cold water until the mixture forms a soft, slightly sticky ball (if it is too wet, add a little more flour).

➡   STEP 3. SEE PAGE 10

8   Put the potatoes into the stew, then shape the dough into eight small balls and sit them on top of the stew. Put large soup bowls to warm on top of the pan, or place them in the oven at the lowest setting, cover with a lid and cook for a further 20 minutes until the dumplings are fluffy and the potatoes are cooked.

9   Carefully lift out the dumplings and potatoes on to a plate with a draining spoon. Mix 2 tbsp plain flour with a little cold water to make a smooth paste. Stir into the stew until it is thickened and bubbling. Add a little gravy block or gravy browning and salt to taste. Take out the bay leaf. Put the potatoes and dumplings back into the stew to reheat for a few minutes.

10 Spoon into the warm soup bowls and serve straight away.

liver and onion hotpot
with golden potato topping

SERVES 4

storecupboard ingredients

frozen peas

butter or margarine

milk

sunflower oil

plain (all-purpose) flour

salt and pepper

dried sage

1 beef stock cube

shopping list

450 g/1 lb pigs' liver

450 g/1 lb potatoes

3 large onions

2 carrots

1 cooking (tart) apple

extra equipment

shallow dish

mixing bowl

grater

large, flameproof casserole (Dutch oven)

draining spoon

measuring jug

top tip!

Try adding half a swede (rutabaga), grated, instead of the carrots.

1   Cut the liver into bite-sized chunks, discarding any gristly bits. Put in a shallow dish and add about 2 tbsp milk. Stir and leave to stand for 15 minutes while preparing the rest of the dish.

2   Peel and slice the potatoes fairly thinly and put in a bowl of cold water to prevent them from browning.

3   Slice the onions.   ➡

4   Peel and grate the carrots on the coarse side of the grater.

5   Cut the apple into quarters, cut out the cores, then peel and slice the quarters.

6   Heat 2 tbsp oil in the casserole dish over a fairly high heat and fry (sauté) the onions, stirring occasionally, for 3 minutes.

7   Lift the onions out of the casserole with a draining spoon and put on a plate.

8   Lift the liver out of the milk and fry it quickly in the casserole, stirring until brown all over. Put the onions back in the casserole.

9   Put 1 tbsp flour in a measuring jug and mix with a little water until smooth. Make up to 450 ml/¾ pt/2 cups with more water. Pour into the casserole and crumble in the stock cube.

10 Stirring all the time, let the mixture bubble until it thickens.

11 Turn the oven on to 190°C/375°F/gas mark 5. Stir the sliced apple, grated carrots and peas, a good sprinkling of dried sage and some salt and pepper into the casserole. Take the potatoes out of the water and arrange overlapping on top. Put tiny pieces of butter or margarine over the surface at intervals. Cover with foil.

12 Bake in the oven for 30 minutes, then take off the foil and cook for a further 30 minutes until the potatoes are turning golden brown. Remember to put some plates in the oven to warm for a few minutes before serving.

➡   STEP 3. SEE PAGE 9

burgundy braised beef
with vegetables and mustard

SERVES 4–6

storecupboard ingredients

butter or margarine

sunflower oil

1 beef stock cube

tomato purée (paste)

1 bay leaf

red Burgundy wine

salt and pepper

mustard

shopping list

1 kg/2¼ lb piece of silverside or topside of beef

1 onion

2 large carrots

1 turnip

4 celery sticks

4 large potatoes

extra equipment

large saucepan or flameproof casserole (Dutch oven)

wineglass

measuring jug

carving dish

top tip!

Any leftover meat is delicious cold with mashed potatoes (see page 43), salad (see page 12) and horseradish-flavoured mayonnaise. To make this, simply mix 4–6 tbsp good-quality mayonnaise with 1 tbsp horseradish sauce.

1   Chop the onion. ➡

2   Dice the carrots, turnip and celery. ➡

3   Melt a knob of butter or margarine and 1 tbsp oil over a high heat in a large saucepan or flameproof casserole. Add the meat and brown quickly on all sides, then lift out of the pan.

4   Add the prepared vegetables and stir over a high heat for 2 minutes.

5   Add 300 ml/½ pt/1¼ cups water. Crumble in the stock cube and stir in a good squeeze of tomato purée. Add a wineglass of red Burgundy, the bay leaf and a sprinkling of salt and pepper. Stir well and put the meat back on top of the vegetables.

6   When the liquid is bubbling rapidly, turn down the heat to very low. Cover tightly with a lid and let it cook very gently for 1½ hours.

7   While it is cooking, peel the potatoes and cut them into quarters. Turn on the oven at its lowest setting and put a carving dish and plates in to warm. Turn the meat over in the pan and arrange the potatoes around. Re-cover and cook for a further 30 minutes or until the meat and potatoes are tender.

8   Lift the meat and potatoes out of the pan on to the carving dish. Slice some of the meat and arrange on the warm plates. Discard the bay leaf, then spoon the diced vegetables and cooking liquid over and put the potato halves to one side. Serve with mustard.

➡ STEP 1. SEE PAGE 9

➡ STEP 2. SEE PAGE 10

spiced persian lamb
with flageolets

SERVES 6

storecupboard ingredients

425 g/15 oz/1 large can of flageolet beans

paprika

ground cumin

ground coriander (cilantro)

ground ginger

sunflower oil

1 vegetable stock cube

1 bouquet garni sachet

tomato purée (paste)

salt and pepper

cornflour (cornstarch)

butter or margarine

shopping list

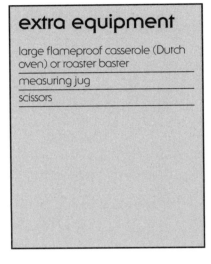

1.6 kg/3½ lb leg of lamb

2 onions

3 carrots

3 celery sticks

3 large potatoes

fresh parsley

extra equipment

large flameproof casserole (Dutch oven) or roaster baster

measuring jug

scissors

1   Wipe the lamb and place in a casserole dish.

2   In a cup, mix 1 tsp each of paprika, cumin and coriander with ½ tsp ginger and some salt and pepper. Sprinkle all over the lamb, cover and leave for at least 2 hours or overnight if you can.

3   Chop the onions and dice the remaining vegetables. ➡ ➡

➡ STEP 3. SEE PAGE 9

4   Lift the lamb out of its dish and heat a knob of butter or margarine and 1 tbsp oil in the dish over a fairly high heat. Brown the lamb on all sides and then lift it out again.

5   Add a further knob of butter or margarine to the pan and fry (sauté) the vegetables for 2 minutes, stirring. Turn off the heat and return the lamb to the dish.

6   Turn on the oven to 180°C/350°F/gas mark 4. Boil a kettle. Measure 300 ml/½ pt/1¼ cups boiling water, stir in the stock cube and a good squeeze of tomato purée and pour around the lamb. Add the bouquet garni sachet. Heat again until the liquid bubbles, then put on the lid and cook in the oven for 1¼ hours.

➡ STEP 3. SEE PAGE 10

7   While the lamb is cooking, peel the potatoes and cut into fairly large chunks. Cover with cold water until ready to use. Drain the can of flageolet beans. After 1¼ hours, stir the beans into the vegetables around the lamb and arrange the potatoes on top. Sprinkle lightly with salt. Re-cover and cook in the oven for a further 45 minutes. Put plates and a carving dish to warm in the oven while the meat finishes cooking.

8   Blend 1 tbsp cornflour with a little water in a cup. Chop a small handful of parsley (see Top Tip page 20). Lift the meat out on to the carving dish with the potatoes. Discard the bouquet garni sachet. Stir the blended cornflour into the vegetables and juices in the pan and cook over a moderate heat until thickened and bubbling. Add salt and pepper to taste.

9   Cut the meat into thick slices (it will be very tender). Put on the warm plates with the potatoes and spoon the thick vegetable mixture over. Sprinkle with parsley and serve.

tyrolean hotpot
with cabbage and caraway

SERVES 4

storecupboard ingredients

sunflower oil

garlic purée (paste)

1 vegetable stock cube

salt and pepper

butter or margarine

shopping list

4 pork shoulder steaks

1 small onion

½ small white cabbage

4 fairly large potatoes

caraway seeds

extra equipment
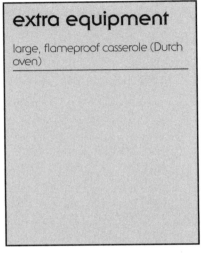

large, flameproof casserole (Dutch oven)

top tip!

Try this with frankfurter sausages instead of pork. There's no need to brown them before cooking.

1   Thinly slice the onion.   ➡

2   Cut out the thick central stalk from the cabbage, then cut the cabbage into thin slices. Separate into shreds.

3   Scrub and thinly slice the potatoes.

4   Heat 2 tbsp oil in a flameproof casserole over a fairly high heat. Add the pork steaks and brown on both sides.

5   Take the steaks out of the pan and put in the onion, a small squeeze of garlic purée and the cabbage and cook, turning and stirring, for 2 minutes until the cabbage is beginning to soften.

6   Pour in 300 ml/½ pt/1¼ cups water and crumble in the stock cube. Cook, stirring all the time, until the liquid is bubbling. Sprinkle with caraway seeds and some salt and pepper.

7   Lay the pork steaks on top, then cover with a layer of overlapping potato slices. Dot the surface with tiny flakes of butter or margarine and sprinkle lightly again with salt and pepper. Cover with a lid or foil and turn the heat down to fairly low.

8   Cook for 25 minutes until everything is tender. Warm your plates on top of the casserole, under the lid, for the last few minutes of cooking time and then serve straight from the pan.

➡ STEP 1. SEE PAGE 9

9 curries and casseroles

Curries are top of many people's lists of favourite meals and casseroles are almost foolproof for novice chefs because you simply throw them together and leave them to cook themselves. I've included chilli con carne in this chapter as it is another popular spiced dish served with rice.

tandoori chicken
with naan bread, cucumber raita and salad

SERVES 4

storecupboard ingredients

garlic purée (paste)

tomato purée

ground ginger

garam masala

paprika

chilli powder

dried mint

shopping list

4 chicken portions (leg and thigh)

450 ml/¾ pt/2 cups plain yoghurt

1 lemon

1 cucumber

1 crisp lettuce

2 tomatoes

1 small onion

4 naan breads

extra equipment

shallow dish

citrus squeezer

egg cup

small bowl

baking (cookie) sheet

small serving bowl

1 Pull all the skin off the chicken. Holding each portion firmly, gently pull the limb until you see where the joint is, then cut through the joint to make two pieces. Place in a shallow dish. Using a sharp knife, make several cuts in the flesh right through to the bone.

2 Cut the lemon in half and squeeze the juice from one half. Cut the other half into four wedges for garnish.

3 Mix two-thirds of the yoghurt with the lemon juice, a small squeeze of garlic purée, a large squeeze of tomato purée, 2 good pinches of ground ginger, 1 tbsp each garam masala and paprika and a good pinch of chilli powder. Spoon all over the chicken pieces and rub in well with the back of a spoon. Cover and chill in the fridge for several hours or, preferably, overnight.

5 When ready to cook, preheat the oven to 200°C/400°F/gas mark 6. Lift the chicken pieces out of the dish and place well apart on a baking sheet. Cook for 20 minutes.

6 While the chicken is cooking, make the cucumber raita. Cut off about a quarter of the cucumber and grate on the coarse side of the grater. Squeeze out most of the moisture with your hand and place the cucumber in a small bowl. Add 2 tsp dried mint and the rest of the yoghurt. Mix well and season with salt and pepper. You can add a tiny squeeze of garlic purée too, if you like. Chill until ready to serve.

7 Remove the baking sheet from the oven and pour off any liquid. Return it to the oven and cook for a further 20 minutes until the chicken is cooked through.

8 Meanwhile, prepare the salad ingredients, but don't put them in a salad bowl or make any dressing. Put the naan breads on the bottom shelf of the hot oven for 3–4 minutes to warm. ➡

9 Put a pile of lettuce on the side of each plate. Arrange cucumber, tomato wedges and onion rings over. Put the naan breads on the plates and top each with two pieces of chicken. Garnish with a wedge of lemon. Serve with the cucumber raita.

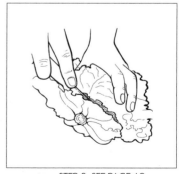

➡ STEP 8. SEE PAGE 12

tandoori fish
with red rice and beans

SERVES 4

storecupboard ingredients

400 g/14 oz/1 large can of chopped tomatoes

lemon juice

ground cumin

ground coriander (cilantro)

ground turmeric

chilli powder

salt

long-grain rice

shopping list

750 g/1½ lb cod or haddock fillet

1 small carton of plain yoghurt

fresh coriander

100 g/4 oz French (green) beans

1 lemon

extra equipment

large shallow dish

baking tin (pan)

scissors

top tip!

Fresh herbs, such as coriander, parsley, basil, mint, etc. can be chopped and frozen for future use.

1   Put the fish on a board, skin-side down. Make a small cut at one end of the fish between the flesh and the skin. Hold the skin firmly between your finger and thumb and scrape and push the flesh off the skin, pulling the skin as you go (see Top Tip page 74). Cut the fish into four pieces.

2   In a large shallow dish, mix the yoghurt with 1 tbsp lemon juice and 1 tsp each of ground cumin and coriander and ½ tsp each of turmeric and chilli powder. Add a good pinch of salt and then turn the fish over in the mixture. Leave to marinate for 2 hours.

3   Turn on the oven to 180°C/350°F/gas mark 4. Lift the fish out of the marinade and place in a baking tin. Bake in the oven for 20 minutes, brushing with the remaining marinade halfway through cooking.

4   While the fish is baking, empty the can of tomatoes into a saucepan with half a canful of water. Put over a high heat until the mixture boils. Add 175 g/6 oz/¾ cup rice and stir well. Cover with a lid, reduce the heat to very low and cook for 10 minutes.

5   Meanwhile, cut both ends off the beans and cut each one into three pieces. Add to the rice after 10 minutes, re-cover, put plates under the lid to warm, and continue to cook for a further 10 minutes until the rice and beans are cooked and the rice has absorbed the liquid.

6   Chop a small handful of fresh coriander (see Top Tip page 20) and add to the rice. Stir well.

7   Pile the rice on to the warm plates and top with the fish. Cut the lemon into wedges and use to garnish the plates.

raj-style beef madras
with coconut, raisins and chutney

SERVES 4

storecupboard ingredients

butter or margarine

madras curry powder

plain (all-purpose) flour

1 beef stock cube

garlic purée (paste)

tomato purée

salt and pepper

mango chutney

long-grain rice, preferably basmati

lemon juice

desiccated (shredded) coconut

raisins

shopping list
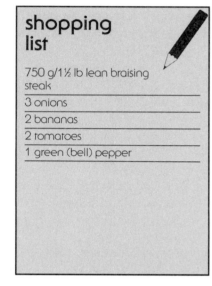

750 g/1½ lb lean braising steak

3 onions

2 bananas

2 tomatoes

1 green (bell) pepper

extra equipment

2 large saucepans

draining spoon

measuring jug

colander

6 small serving bowls, for accompaniments

1   Cut the meat into bite-sized pieces, discarding any fat or gristle. Heat a large knob of butter or margarine in a saucepan. Add the meat and fry (sauté), stirring, over a high heat, until lightly coloured. Lift out with a draining spoon and put on a plate.

2   Slice the onions. Put half in a small bowl and cover with clingfilm (plastic wrap).   ➡

➡ STEP 2. SEE PAGE 9

3   Put the rest of the onion into the saucepan and fry for 3 minutes. Add 1–2 tbsp curry powder and 1 tbsp flour and stir for 2 minutes.

4   Take the pan off the heat. Measure 300 ml/½ pt/1¼ cups water and gradually stir it into the mixture. Crumble in the stock cube, and add a small squeeze of garlic purée, a good squeeze of tomato purée, salt and pepper and 2 tbsp mango chutney. Return the mixture to the heat and cook, stirring until it thickens.

5   Put the meat back into the sauce. Heat until boiling, then turn the heat down as low as it will go. Cover and leave to cook very gently for 2½ hours, stirring occasionally. If the meat looks as though it is getting too dry, add a little more water.

6   When the curry has been cooking for 2 hours, cook the rice.   ➡

➡ STEP 6. SEE PAGE 14

7   Put four plates on top of the curry pan, under the lid, to warm.

8   Peel and slice the bananas into a small serving bowl. Sprinkle all over with lemon juice – this will prevent browning.

9   Prepare the tomato and green pepper and put into another small bowl.   ➡

10 Put desiccated coconut, raisins and mango chutney into three other bowls.

11 Spoon the rice on the warm plates, top with the curry and serve with the accompaniments.

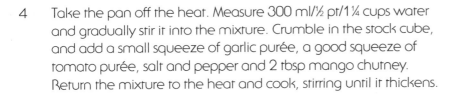

➡ STEP 9. SEE PAGE 12

keema curry
with cardamom rice

SERVES 4

storecupboard ingredients

sunflower oil

curry powder

ground ginger

tomato purée (paste)

garlic purée

long-grain rice, preferably basmati

mango chutney

salt

frozen peas

shopping list

450 g/1 lb minced (ground) beef

2 onions

whole cardamom pods

extra equipment

2 large saucepans

measuring jug

colander

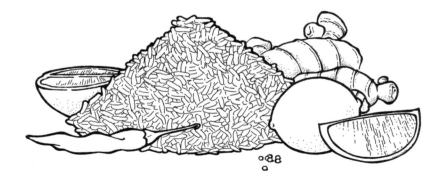

1   Chop the onions.   ➡

2   Heat 2 tbsp oil in a large saucepan over a moderate heat. Add the onions and cook, stirring, for 3 minutes until the onions are transparent but not browned.

3   Add the minced beef and cook, stirring, for 5 minutes until the meat is browned all over and all the grains are separate.

4   Add 2 tbsp curry powder and stir for 1 minute. Add 1 tsp ground ginger, a small squeeze of garlic purée, 300 ml/½ pt/1¼ cups water, a handful of frozen peas and a good squeeze of tomato purée. Stir well and bring it up to the boil. Turn down the heat and leave it to cook for 30 minutes, stirring occasionally. Put plates to warm over the pan for the last few minutes.

5   While the curry is cooking, cook the rice, adding 8 cardamom pods to the boiling water.   ➡

6   Taste the curry and season with salt.

7   Spoon the rice on to the warm plates, add the curry and serve with mango chutney.

➡ STEP 1. SEE PAGE 9

➡ STEP 5. SEE PAGE 14

eastern lamb
with onion rice

SERVES 4

storecupboard ingredients

225g/8 oz cooked leftover lamb

garlic purée (paste)

ground ginger

ground cumin

ground coriander (cilantro)

ground turmeric

salt and pepper

sunflower oil

long-grain rice, preferably basmati

flaked (slivered) almonds

raisins

desiccated (shredded) coconut

mango chutney

shopping list

1 small carton of plain yoghurt

2 onions

100 g/4 oz French (green) beans

extra equipment

medium saucepan

large saucepan

frying pan (skillet)

top tip!

This can also be made with raw chicken breast, cut into bite-sized pieces.

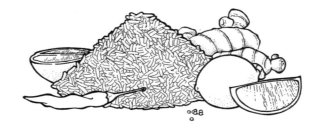

1   Cut the lamb into bite-sized pieces, discarding any fat.

2   Put a small squeeze of garlic purée into a medium-sized saucepan. Add 1 tsp each of ginger, cumin, coriander and turmeric. Stir in the yoghurt and a sprinkling of salt and pepper.

3   Stir in the lamb and leave to stand for 10 minutes.

4   Meanwhile, slice the onion. ➡

5   Cut both ends off the beans and cut each one into three pieces.

6   Put the lamb over a moderate heat and cook for about 20 minutes, stirring occasionally (the mixture will curdle and look watery at first and then will gradually dry out).

7   Cook the rice, adding 1 tsp turmeric to the water. Add the beans after 5 minutes' cooking time. ➡

8   Turn on the oven at the lowest setting and put in plates to warm. Meanwhile, heat 2 tbsp oil in a frying pan. Add the sliced onion and fry (sauté) for 5 minutes over a fairly high heat until golden brown. Remove from the pan with a draining spoon and drain on kitchen paper (paper towels).

9   Add a small handful of raisins and almonds to the frying pan and fry, stirring, until the nuts are brown. Remove from the heat immediately or they will burn.

10 Stir the fried onions into the drained rice. Pile the rice on to the warmed plates and spoon the lamb mixture on top. Sprinkle with coconut and the fried raisins and almonds. Serve with mango chutney.

➡ STEP 4. SEE PAGE 9

➡ STEP 7. SEE PAGE 14

chilli con carne
with boiled rice

SERVES 4

storecupboard ingredients

425g/15 oz/1 large can of red kidney beans

400 g/14 oz/1 large can of chopped tomatoes

chilli powder

ground cumin

dried oregano

salt and pepper

tomato purée (paste)

long-grain rice

Cheddar cheese

shopping list

350 g/12 oz minced (ground) beef

1 onion

1 iceberg lettuce

extra equipment

2 large saucepans

colander

grater

top tip!

Instead of serving with rice, for a change spoon the Chilli con Carne on to warmed flour tortillas, top with lettuce and cheese and roll up; or put in crispy taco shells and then top with the lettuce and cheese. The addition of a little tomato or chilli relish is a good idea too.

1   Put a large saucepan of water on to boil and add 1 tsp salt.

2   Chop the onion.   ➡

3   Place the onion in another large saucepan with the minced beef. Cook over a high heat, stirring all the time, until the meat is no longer pink and all the grains are separate.

➡ STEP 2. SEE PAGE 9

4   Add ½ tsp chilli powder (or to taste) and the same of ground cumin. Stir for 1 minute.

5   Add the contents of the can of beans (including the liquid) and the contents of the can of tomatoes. Stir well.

6   Sprinkle a little dried oregano over the surface with some salt and pepper and a good squeeze of tomato purée. Stir well and heat until the mixture bubbles.

7   Turn the heat down to low and let it simmer very gently. Stir once or twice to prevent sticking.

8   While the chilli is simmering, cook the rice in the pan of boiling water.   ➡

➡ STEP 8. SEE PAGE 14

9   When the rice is nearly cooked, put four plates to warm on top of the pan of chilli. Cut the iceberg lettuce in half. Put one half in the fridge for use on another occasion. Slice the other half into thin shreds.

10 Grate a good chunk of cheese on the coarse side of a cheese grater.

11 Spoon the cooked rice into nests on the warm plates. Spoon the chilli into the centre and serve with lots of shredded lettuce and grated cheese.

rich beef and tomato casserole
with jacket potatoes and baked courgettes

SERVES 4

storecupboard ingredients

400 g/14 oz/1 large can of chopped tomatoes

plain (all-purpose) flour

salt and pepper

tomato purée (paste)

garlic purée

olive oil

dried basil

shopping list

450 g/1 lb diced braising steak

1 small carton soured (dairy sour) cream

1 large onion

4 large potatoes

3 large courgettes (zucchini)

extra equipment

flameproof casserole (Dutch oven)

small roasting tin (pan)

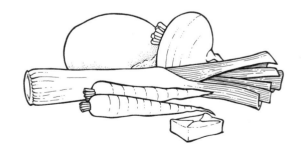

top tip!

If you don't like courgettes, try baking a mixture of thinly sliced carrots and parsnips in the same way.

1   Chop the onion.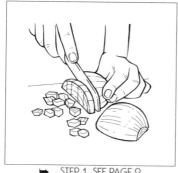

2   Scrub the potatoes and prick all over with a fork.

3   Preheat the oven to 160°C/325°F/gas mark 3.

4   Put the meat in a plastic bag with 4 tbsp flour and a little salt and pepper. Hold the bag firmly and shake to coat the meat in the flour.

5   Heat 3 tbsp oil in a flameproof casserole dish over a fairly high heat. Add the onion and the meat and fry (sauté), stirring all the time, until the meat is browned on all sides.

6   Add the can of tomatoes, a good squeeze of tomato purée and a small squeeze of garlic purée. Stir well and continue to heat until it is bubbling.

7   Stir in 1 tsp dried basil and add another good sprinkling of salt and pepper.

8   Cover with a lid and place on the centre shelf of the oven. Put the potatoes on the same shelf. Cook for 2 hours.

9   While the casserole is cooking, slice the courgettes, discarding the ends. Put enough olive oil in a roasting tin just to cover the base. Add a small squeeze of garlic purée and a pinch of salt and stir to mix. Put in the courgettes and turn over in the oil to coat completely.

10 Place the courgettes on the shelf near the top of the oven above the casserole and potatoes and cook for the remaining casserole cooking time. Put plates in to warm for the last few minutes.

11 Stir the casserole, spoon a little soured cream on top and serve with the jacket potatoes and the courgettes.

➡ STEP 1. SEE PAGE 9

chicken in red wine
with sesame seed potatoes and mangetout

SERVES 4–6

storecupboard ingredients

butter or margarine

olive or sunflower oil

1 bouquet garni sachet

salt and pepper

plain (all-purpose) flour

red wine

shopping list
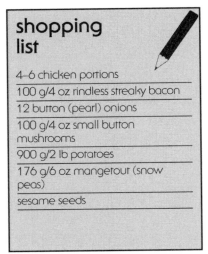

4–6 chicken portions

100 g/4 oz rindless streaky bacon

12 button (pearl) onions

100 g/4 oz small button mushrooms

900 g/2 lb potatoes

176 g/6 oz mangetout (snow peas)

sesame seeds

extra equipment

scissors

large frying pan (skillet)

draining spoon

large casserole dish (Dutch oven)

measuring jug

roasting tin (pan)

small saucepan

colander

top tip!

This recipe can be adapted to make Chicken Véronique: omit the bacon, use white wine instead of red and add 100 g/4 oz halved, green seedless grapes and 3 tbsp single (light) cream to the sauce, just before serving.

1   Pull the skin off the chicken. Snip the bacon into small pieces. Peel the onions and leave whole. Wipe the mushrooms.

2   Melt a good knob of butter or margarine and 1 tbsp oil in a large frying pan. Add the chicken and brown all over. Lift out of the pan and put in the casserole dish.

3   Add the bacon and onions to the frying pan and fry (sauté) quickly, stirring for 2 minutes. Transfer to the casserole with a draining spoon and add the mushrooms with the bouquet garni sachet.

4   Turn the oven on to 190°C/375°F/gas mark 5. Blend 3 tbsp flour with a little water in a measuring jug. Gradually stir in half the bottle of red wine. Pour into the frying pan and cook, stirring until thick and bubbling. Pour into the casserole. Season, cover with a lid and cook in the centre of the oven for 1¼ hours.

5   As soon as the chicken is in the oven, scrub the potatoes and cut each one into 4–6 pieces, depending on size.

6   Pour enough olive or sunflower oil in a roasting tin to cover the base. Turn the potatoes in the oil to coat completely. Sprinkle with salt and a small handful of sesame seeds. Put on the top shelf of the oven, above the casserole, and cook for about 1 hour until browned and cooked through.

7   About 15 minutes before the chicken will be cooked, put serving dishes and plates in the oven to warm.

8   Heat about 1 cm/½ in water in a small saucepan with a pinch of salt. Cut the stalks off the mangetout. When the water is boiling, add the mangetout, cover with a lid and cook for about 4 minutes until tender. Drain in a colander in the sink, then put in a warmed serving dish in the oven.

9   Using a draining spoon, transfer the potatoes to a warmed serving dish and keep warm. Remove the casserole from the oven, stir and discard the bouquet garni. Taste and season, if necessary. Serve with the sesame seed potatoes and the mangetout.

sherried chicken casserole
with jacket potatoes and peas

SERVES 4

storecupboard ingredients

400 g/14 oz/1 large can of chopped tomatoes

sunflower oil

1 chicken stock cube

dried mixed herbs

dry sherry or vermouth

salt and pepper

frozen peas

butter or margarine

shopping list

1 onion

4 chicken portions

100 g/4 oz button mushrooms

4 large potatoes

extra equipment

large, flameproof casserole (Dutch oven)

2 metal skewers

small saucepan

colander

top tip!

Use any frozen vegetable you have to hand as a quick accompaniment to any main dish. Contrary to popular belief, they are very good for you!

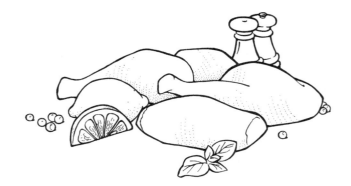

1   Chop the onion. ➡

➡   STEP 1. SEE PAGE 9

2   Wipe the mushrooms to remove any soil, then cut into halves or quarters, if large.

3   Turn on the oven to 180°C/350°F/gas mark 4. Heat about 3 tbsp oil in the casserole over a fairly high heat. Add the onion and fry (sauté) for 2 minutes, stirring. Add the chicken, skin-sides down and brown for 3–4 minutes, turning once.

4   Add the mushrooms.

5   Open the can of tomatoes and pour all over the chicken. Add a good slosh of sherry or vermouth and crumble in the stock cube round the sides. Sprinkle mixed herbs, salt and pepper lightly over the surface. Wait until the liquid is bubbling, then cover with a lid. Put in the oven and cook for 1½ hours.

6   As soon as the chicken is in the oven, scrub the potatoes and prick all over with a fork. Thread two potatoes on each of two metal skewers. Place in the oven either on the same shelf as the casserole or above it.

7   About 15 minutes before the casserole is due to be ready, put plates to warm in the oven and put about 1 cm/½ in water in a small saucepan. Place over a fairly high heat and add a pinch of salt. When the water boils, add a handful of peas per person. Cover with a lid and cook for 5 minutes. Drain in a colander in the sink, then rest the colander over the saucepan and cover.

8   Take the potatoes out of the oven and slide them off the skewers. Make a cross-cut in the top of each and squeeze gently to open slightly. Put on the warm plates and add a small knob of butter or margarine to each. Serve the casserole with the jacket potatoes and peas.

chicken and mushroom casserole
with oven-cooked vegetable rice

SERVES 4

storecupboard ingredients

298 g/10¾ oz/1 medium can of condensed cream of mushroom soup

plain (all-purpose) flour

salt and pepper

sunflower oil

curry powder

long-grain rice

1 chicken stock cube

frozen peas

butter or margarine

shopping list

4 chicken portions

100 g/4 oz button mushrooms

2 carrots

extra equipment

2 flameproof casseroles (Dutch ovens)

grater

measuring jug

top tip!

You can vary the flavour of the rice by adding a small grated parsnip or piece of grated swede (rutabaga) instead of one of the carrots.

1   Pull most of the skin off the chicken. Mix 2 tbsp flour with a little salt and pepper in a plastic bag. Add one chicken portion at a time and shake the bag to coat the portion in flour.

2   Wipe the mushrooms to remove any soil and cut into slices. Turn on the oven to 180°C/350°F/gas mark 4.

3   Heat 2 tbsp oil in a casserole dish over a fairly high heat. Add the chicken and brown all over. Lift out of the casserole and put on a plate.

4   Turn down the heat to moderate. Add 1 tsp curry powder and the mushrooms and cook, stirring, for 1 minute.

5   Stir in the can of soup and wait until it bubbles. Return the chicken to the casserole and turn over in the sauce. Cover with a lid and cook on the shelf below the centre of the oven for 2 hours.

6   When the chicken has been cooking for about an hour, peel and grate the carrots on the coarse side of a grater.

7   Heat a knob of butter or margarine in another casserole dish over a moderate heat. Measure 225 g/8 oz/1 cup rice and stir into the casserole until every grain is glistening. Stir in the carrots and two handfuls of peas.

8   Add 600 ml/1 pt/2½ cups water and crumble in the stock cube. Turn up the heat and stir until bubbling. Sprinkle with salt and pepper. Cover with a lid and transfer to the shelf above the centre of the oven. Cook for 20 minutes – no longer. Put the plates to warm in the oven for the last few minutes.

9   Remove the rice from the oven, lift off the lid and stir gently with a fork. Spoon the rice on to the warm plates and top with the chicken and sauce.

10 pasta and rice dishes

Pasta and rice dishes are economical, filling, tasty and nutritious. They are great for everyday eating or for entertaining and most people love them!

The most important thing when cooking pasta and rice, however, is not to overcook them. Sticky and soggy means unappetising and pushed to the side of the plate. So follow the step-by-step instructions on pages 14 and 15 for perfect results every time.

spaghetti bolognese
with a mixed salad

SERVES 4

storecupboard ingredients

400 g/14 oz/1 large can of chopped tomatoes

tomato purée (paste)

garlic purée

dried oregano

salt and pepper

olive oil

red wine vinegar

spaghetti

grated Parmesan cheese

shopping list

350 g/12 oz minced (ground) lamb or beef

2 onions

1 lettuce

½ cucumber

2 tomatoes

extra equipment

large saucepan

medium saucepan

colander

1   Put the water on to boil for the spaghetti.   ➡

2   Chop one of the onions.   ➡

3   Put in a medium-sized saucepan with the meat. Cook over a
    fairly high heat, stirring all the time until the meat is no longer
    pink and all the grains are separate.

4   Add the can of tomatoes, a good squeeze of tomato purée and a
    small squeeze of garlic purée. Stir well. Sprinkle a little salt, pepper
    and dried oregano over and stir again.

5   When the mixture is boiling hard, turn down the heat until it is
    only just bubbling, stir again and leave to cook while you prepare
    the rest of the meal.

6   Now cook your spaghetti.   ➡

7   While it is cooking, turn on the oven at the lowest setting and
    put plates in to warm. Make a mixed salad and French
    dressing.   ➡   ➡

8   Use spaghetti tongs or a large spoon and fork to transfer the
    cooked spaghetti to the warm plates. Spoon the Bolognese sauce
    over and sprinkle with grated Parmesan cheese. Serve with the
    salad.

➡   STEPS 1 and 6. SEE PAGE 15

➡   STEP 2. SEE PAGE 9

➡   STEP 7. SEE PAGE 12

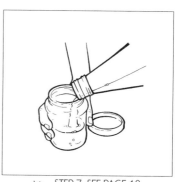

➡   STEP 7. SEE PAGE 13

sausage pasta bake
with basil tomatoes

SERVES 4

storecupboard ingredients

400 g/14 oz/1 large can of tomatoes

tagliatelle

garlic purée (paste)

plain (all-purpose) flour

dried sage

dried basil

cornflakes

salt and pepper

butter or margarine

milk

Cheddar cheese

shopping list

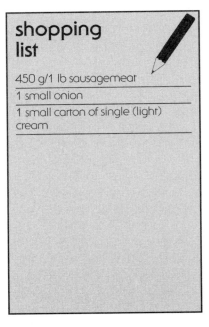

450 g/1 lb sausagemeat

1 small onion

1 small carton of single (light) cream

extra equipment

large saucepan

frying pan (skillet)

fish slice

grater

large shallow ovenproof serving dish

small casserole (Dutch oven)

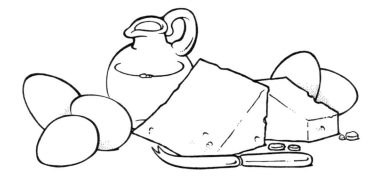

1   Measure out 175 g/6 oz pasta and cook. Once drained, return the pasta to the saucepan. ➡

2   While the pasta is cooking, divide the sausagemeat into walnut-sized pieces. Sprinkle your hands with flour and roll into balls.

3   Turn on the oven to 190°C/375°F/gas mark 5.

4   Finely chop the onion. ➡

5   Grate enough Cheddar cheese on the coarse side of a grater to make about two handfuls of grated cheese.

6   Heat a frying pan, add the sausage balls and fry (sauté) on all sides until brown. Remove from the pan and drain on kitchen paper (paper towels).

7   Add the onion to the pan with a small squeeze of garlic purée and fry, stirring occasionally, for 2 minutes.

8   In a small cup or bowl, mix 1 tbsp flour with 2 tbsp milk until smooth. Stir in the cream, some salt and pepper and ½ tsp each of dried sage and basil. Pour into the frying pan and cook, stirring, for 2 minutes until smooth, thickened and well blended. Stir in one handful of cheese.

9   Pour over the tagliatelle and mix well. Tip into an ovenproof dish and scatter the sausage balls over the top. Crush two handfuls of cornflakes and mix with the remaining grated cheese. Sprinkle over the top and place in the oven near the top.

10 Empty the can of tomatoes into a casserole dish (Dutch oven) and sprinkle with a little dried basil, salt and pepper. Stir gently. Cover and place in the oven below the pasta. Cook for a further 25 minutes until the top of the pasta is golden and bubbling. Warm your plates in the oven for the last few minutes of cooking time. Serve the pasta with the tomatoes.

➡ STEP 1. SEE PAGE 15

➡ STEP 4. SEE PAGE 9

lasagne al forno
with italian salad

SERVES 4

storecupboard ingredients

400 g/14 oz/1 large can of chopped tomatoes

no-need-to-precook lasagne sheets

tomato purée (paste)

garlic purée

dried oregano

salt and pepper

caster (superfine) sugar

red wine (optional)

olive oil

red wine vinegar

plain (all-purpose) flour

butter or margarine

Cheddar cheese

milk

shopping list

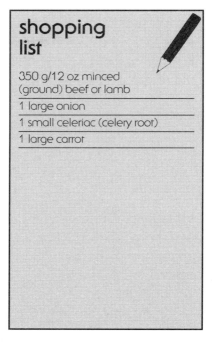

350 g/12 oz minced (ground) beef or lamb

1 large onion

1 small celeriac (celery root)

1 large carrot

extra equipment

large saucepan

smaller saucepan

balloon whisk

grater

shallow ovenproof dish

salad bowl

1   Make the meat sauce. Begin by finely chopping the onion. ➡

2   Put half of it in a large saucepan with the minced meat. Cook over a fairly high heat, stirring all the time until the meat is no longer pink and all the grains are separate.

3   Add the contents of the can of tomatoes, a good squeeze of tomato purée, a small squeeze of garlic purée, a good sprinkling each of dried oregano and caster sugar and some salt and pepper. Stir well. Add a good slosh of red wine, if liked. Let the mixture boil rapidly, then turn down the heat, stir well again and leave to bubble gently for 15 minutes.

4   While the meat sauce is cooking, make a basic white sauce. ➡

5   Grate some Cheddar cheese until you have two good handfuls. Put about two-thirds of the cheese into the sauce and stir well.

6   Turn on the oven to 190°C/375°F/gas mark 5.

7   Put a little of the meat mixture in the base of a shallow ovenproof dish and spread it out (it doesn't have to cover the base completely).

8   Cover with a layer of lasagne sheets, breaking them to fit, if necessary. Cover with about half the remaining meat mixture, then a further layer of lasagne. Repeat the layers again.

9   Spoon the cheese sauce over the top and sprinkle with the remaining grated cheese. Bake in the oven for 40 minutes until the top is bubbling and golden brown.

10 About 15 minutes before the end of cooking time, put in the plates to warm. Peel the skin off the celeriac and the carrot. Grate them on the coarse side of the grater. Put in a salad bowl with the remaining chopped onion. Make some French dressing. ➡

11 Add about 4 tbsp French dressing to the Italian salad and mix well. Serve the lasagne on the warm plates with the salad separately.

➡ STEP 1. SEE PAGE 9

➡ STEP 4. SEE PAGE 14

➡ STEP 10. SEE PAGE 13

tuna and sweetcorn pasta
with garlic bread and a green salad

SERVES 4

storecupboard ingredients

185 g/6½ oz/1 small can of tuna

200 g/7 oz/1 small can of sweetcorn (corn)

penne or other pasta shapes

plain (all-purpose) flour

garlic purée (paste)

olive oil

wine vinegar

salt and pepper

caster (superfine) sugar

milk

butter or margarine

Cheddar cheese

shopping list

1 small French stick

1 lettuce

1 cucumber

1 green (bell) pepper

1 box of cress

fresh parsley

extra equipment

large saucepan

small saucepan

balloon whisk

measuring jug

grater

salad bowl

top tip!

If you don't want to put the oven on, make garlic slices under the grill. Simply prepare as for garlic bread (see page 13) but cut the slices right through and spread each with the garlic butter. Put the slices under a hot grill (broiler) until the butter melts and the bread is browning at the edges but is still soft.

1   Put a large pan of water on to boil to cook the pasta. While the water is coming to the boil, before adding the pasta, prepare the garlic bread. ➡

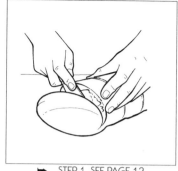

➡ STEP 1. SEE PAGE 13

2   Cook 175 g/6 oz pasta shapes. ➡

3   When the pasta and garlic bread are cooking, make a basic white sauce. ➡

4   Drain the pasta and return it to the saucepan.

5   Grate some Cheddar cheese so you have a good handful. Add to the sauce.

6   Drain off the liquid from the tuna and the sweetcorn. Stir the fish and the sweetcorn into the sauce with a wooden spoon.

➡ STEP 2. SEE PAGE 15

7   Put the plates to warm in the oven. Prepare a green salad. ➡

8   Add the tuna and sweetcorn sauce to the pan of drained pasta and cook, stirring continuously, over a gentle heat until piping hot.

9   Spoon the pasta on to the warm plates and garnish with parsley sprigs. Serve with the hot garlic bread and the green salad.

STEP 3, PAGE 14

STEP 7, PAGE 16

spaghetti carbonara
with mixed salad

SERVES 4

storecupboard ingredients

spaghetti

olive oil

garlic purée (paste)

salt and pepper

wine vinegar

caster (superfine) sugar

2 eggs

milk or single (light) cream

shopping list

6 rashers (slices) of rindless streaky bacon

2 onions

fresh parsley

1 lettuce

2 tomatoes

1 cucumber

1 red (bell) pepper

extra equipment

large saucepan

small saucepan

scissors

spoon and fork or tongs

salad bowl

top tip!

You can add sliced mushrooms to the bacon mixture or use chopped ham instead of bacon for a change.

1   Put a large pan of water on to boil to cook the spaghetti.   ➡

2   While the water is coming to the boil, before adding the spaghetti, chop one onion for the carbonara (keep the other one for the salad) and cut the bacon into small pieces with scissors.   ➡

3   Cook the spaghetti.   ➡

4   While it is boiling, heat 4 tbsp olive oil in a small saucepan. Add the chopped onion and the bacon and cook, stirring, for 3 minutes over a fairly low heat until the onion is transparent but not brown and the bacon is cooked.

5   Add a good squeeze of garlic purée, stir, cover with a lid, turn the heat down as low as possible and leave to cook until the spaghetti is ready.

6   Chop a small handful of parsley (see Top Tip page 22) and add to the bacon and onions. Put plates over the pan with the saucepan lid on top to warm.

7   Make a mixed salad.   ➡

8   When you have drained the spaghetti, put it back in the saucepan. Add the contents of the smaller pan and stir well.

9   Break 2 eggs into a cup and beat with a fork until well blended. Beat in about 3 tbsp milk or single cream and some salt and pepper.

10 Pour this mixture into the spaghetti and put over a gentle heat. Cook, stirring until the egg mixture is just beginning to scramble but the mixture is still creamy. Take off the heat immediately.

11 Pile on to the warmed plates using a fork and spoon or tongs and serve with the salad.

➡   STEPS 1 and 3. SEE PAGE 15

➡   STEP 2. SEE PAGE 9

➡   STEP 7. SEE PAGE 12

smoked haddock kedgeree
with glazed carrots

SERVES 4

storecupboard ingredients

long-grain rice

ground turmeric

salt and pepper

cayenne

paprika

caster (superfine) sugar

frozen peas

3 eggs

butter

milk or single (light) cream

shopping list

225 g/8 oz smoked haddock

450 g/1 lb carrots

fresh parsley

extra equipment

2 large saucepans

colander

frying pan (skillet)

measuring jug

scissors

top tip!
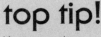

You can make an equally delicious white fish kedgeree by substituting plain cod or haddock for the smoked variety and omitting the ground turmeric.

1   Cook 225 g/8 oz/1 cup rice. Add a good shake of turmeric and a handful of frozen peas to the rice halfway through cooking. Drain in a colander and return to the saucepan. ➡

2   While the rice is cooking, dice the carrots. ➡

3   Melt a large knob of butter in a frying pan. Add the carrots and turn over in the butter until coated. Add 150 ml/¼ pt/⅔ cup water, sprinkle liberally with caster sugar and add just a pinch of salt. When the mixture is bubbling, turn down the heat to low, cover with a lid and leave to cook for about 15 minutes until the carrots are tender.

➡ STEP 1. SEE PAGE 14

4   Put the fish in another saucepan and cover with water. Scrub the eggs under cold running water and add to the pan. Put over a high heat. When the water is bubbling rapidly, turn down the heat to moderate, cover with plates (to warm) and a lid, and cook for 10 minutes. Remove the plates, lift out the eggs and place them in cold water. Lift out the fish, and put it on a board or plate.

5   Pull the skin off the fish and break the flesh into chunks. Add to the cooked rice.

➡ STEP 2. SEE PAGE 10

6   Tap the shells of the eggs on the work surface and then peel off the shells. Cut the eggs into chunks and add to the rice and fish. Check the carrots and, if they are cooked, leave the lid off and turn up the heat to boil off any remaining liquid, then turn off the heat.

7   Chop the parsley (see Top Tip page 20). Add to the rice with a good pinch of cayenne and some salt and pepper. Add a little milk or single cream to moisten the mixture and stir over a gentle heat until very hot throughout.

8   Spoon on to the warm plates, sprinkle with paprika and serve with the glazed carrots.

smoked ham and mushroom risotto
with sautéed courgettes

SERVES 4

storecupboard ingredients

arborio (risotto) rice

2 chicken stock cubes

olive oil

salt and pepper

butter or margarine

grated Parmesan cheese

shopping list

100 g/4 oz smoked ham

1 small carton of single (light) cream

1 small onion

100 g/4 oz button mushrooms

3 courgettes (zucchini)

fresh parsley

extra equipment

flameproof casserole (Dutch oven)

measuring jug

frying pan (skillet)

fish slice

top tip!

Arborio rice will give you a really creamy, authentic Italian risotto but you can use ordinary long-grain rice if you prefer.

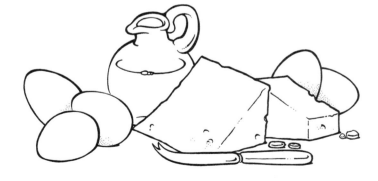

1   Boil a kettle of water. Chop the onion.   ➡

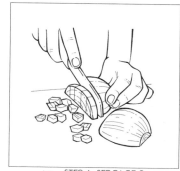

➡ STEP 1. SEE PAGE 9

2   Wipe the mushrooms with a damp cloth to remove any soil, then cut into slices. Cut the ham into small dice.

3   Weigh out 225 g/8 oz/1 cup rice. Add 2 chicken stock cubes to 600 ml/1 pt/2½ cups boiling water and stir until dissolved.

4   Heat a good knob of butter or margarine and 1 tbsp olive oil in a flameproof casserole over a moderate heat.

5   Add the onion and cook for 2 minutes, stirring.

6   Stir in the rice until all the grains are glistening. Stir in the mushrooms.

7   Add half the stock and let it come to the boil. Turn down the heat and let it simmer until the liquid is absorbed.

8   While the rice cooks, cut the ends off the courgettes and cut into fairly thin slices.

9   Heat a good knob of butter or margarine and 2 tbsp olive oil in a frying pan. Add the courgettes and fry (sauté), stirring and turning over occasionally until golden. Transfer to a serving dish lined with kitchen paper (paper towels) and keep warm in the oven at its lowest setting. Put the plates in to warm too.

10   When the rice has absorbed the stock in the casserole, add the remaining stock, stir, turn up the heat until it boils again, then turn down the heat and let it cook gently until all the liquid is absorbed and the rice is just cooked.

11   Stir in the ham and 4 tbsp cream. Taste and season as necessary with salt and pepper. Let it heat for 3 minutes.

12   Spoon on to the warm plates, garnish with sprigs of parsley and serve with the courgettes.

majorcan rice
with green salad and garlic and herb bread

SERVES 4

storecupboard ingredients

long-grain rice

2 chicken stock cubes

salt and pepper

olive oil

garlic purée (paste)

dried mixed herbs

wine vinegar

caster (superfine) sugar

butter or margarine

shopping list

225 g/8 oz chicken stir-fry meat

100 g/4 oz peeled prawns (shrimp)

1 small packet of frozen peas and sweetcorn (corn)

2 green (bell) peppers

1 red pepper

1 lettuce

1 cucumber

1 small jar or can of stoned (pitted) black olives

1 small French stick

extra equipment

measuring jug

large frying pan (skillet)

salad bowl

1   Boil a kettle of water. Dice the red pepper and one of the 2 green peppers. ➡

2   Measure 600 ml/1 pt/2½ cups boiling water and stir in 2 chicken stock cubes until dissolved.

3   Weigh out 225 g/8 oz/1 cup rice.

4   Heat 2 tbsp olive oil in a large frying pan. Add the chicken and chopped peppers and fry (sauté) for 4 minutes over a fairly high heat, stirring all the time.

5   Add the rice and cook for 1 minute, stirring.

6   Keep stirring while you pour on the stock. When the mixture is bubbling rapidly, turn down the heat to low, cover with a lid or foil and cook gently for 10 minutes.

7   Meanwhile, make the garlic and herb bread, adding 2 tsp dried mixed herbs when mashing the butter and garlic. ➡

8   Add about half the packet of peas and sweetcorn (put the rest back in the freezer for use another time) and all the prawns to the rice, stir, re-cover and cook for a further 10 minutes.

9   While the rice cooks, prepare the green salad. Put the plates in the oven briefly to warm. ➡

10 Taste and season the rice with salt and pepper. Scatter as many olives as you like over the surface.

11 Serve the rice straight from the pan with the garlic and herb bread and a green salad.

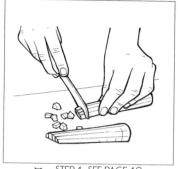

➡ STEP 1. SEE PAGE 10

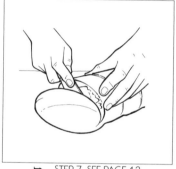

➡ STEP 7. SEE PAGE 13

➡ STEP 9. SEE PAGE 12

chicken and mushroom pilaff
with garlic bread

SERVES 4

storecupboard ingredients

175 g/6 oz leftover cooked chicken

garlic purée (paste)

sunflower oil

wild rice mix

1 vegetable stock cube

1 bay leaf

dried thyme

salt and pepper

frozen peas

butter or margarine

shopping list

1 onion

100 g/4 oz oyster mushrooms

100 g/4 oz chestnut mushrooms

100 g/4 oz button mushrooms

1 small French stick

extra equipment

large saucepan

measuring jug

top tip!

For vegetarians, omit the chicken altogether and serve the pilaff sprinkled with a handful each of grated Mozzarella and Cheddar cheese, mixed.

1   Chop the onion. ➡

2   Wipe the chestnut and button mushrooms to remove any soil. Cut all the mushrooms into slices.

3   Cut the chicken into neat pieces and put to one side to add later.

4   Measure out 175 g/6 oz/¾ cup wild rice mix. Heat about 1 tbsp oil in a large saucepan over a fairly high heat. Add the onion and fry (sauté), stirring for 2 minutes, until lightly coloured.

5   Add the rice and stir for 1 minute until coated in the oil. Measure out 450 ml/¾ pt/2 cups water and add to the rice. Crumble in the stock cube and stir until dissolved. Heat until the water is bubbling.

6   Add the mushrooms, a bay leaf, a sprinkling of dried thyme and salt and pepper. Cover tightly with a lid and turn down the heat to low. Leave to cook for 10 minutes.

7   Make the garlic bread or, if you prefer, make garlic slices (see Top Tip page 112). Put plates to warm in the oven. ➡

8   Remove the lid from the rice, add the chicken and two good handfuls of peas. Cover with a lid again and cook for a further 10 minutes. Remove the lid. The rice should have absorbed all the liquid. If any remains, turn up the heat and cook quickly for a minute or two, stirring gently.

9   Remove the bay leaf, then serve the pilaff on the warm plates with the garlic bread.

➡   STEP 1. SEE PAGE 9

➡   STEP 7. SEE PAGE 13

special prawn fried rice
with chinese salad

SERVES 4

storecupboard ingredients

100 g/4 oz leftover cooked pork or chicken

long-grain rice

sunflower oil

ground turmeric

soy sauce

white wine vinegar

frozen peas

3 eggs

shopping list

100 g/4 oz peeled prawns (shrimp)

125 g/4½ oz packet of beansprouts

1 bunch of spring onions (scallions)

1 green (bell) pepper

1 large carrot

extra equipment

large saucepan

large frying pan (skillet) or wok

grater

small mixing bowl

salad bowl

1   Cook 175 g/6 oz/¾ cup rice, adding a good handful of frozen peas for the last 5 minutes' cooking time. ➡

➡   STEP 1. SEE PAGE 14

2   While the rice is cooking, cut the roots off the spring onions and peel off the outer damaged layers. Cut off about half the green tops. Cut the onions into short lengths.

3   Cut the green pepper in half, remove the stalk, core and seeds and cut one half into small pieces. Cut the other half into thin strips and put in the salad bowl.

4   Cut the pork or chicken into small pieces.

5   Peel the carrot and grate on the coarse side of the grater and add to the salad bowl. Add the beansprouts, a sprinkling of oil, vinegar and soy sauce and toss gently. Leave to stand while preparing the rice dish.

6   Break the eggs into a small mixing bowl and beat with a fork until well blended. Turn on the oven at the lowest setting and put the plates in to warm.

7   Heat 2 tbsp oil in a large frying pan or wok. Fry (sauté) the spring onions and small pieces of pepper for 2 minutes. Add the rice and a sprinkling of turmeric and keep stirring with a fork for 1 minute.

8   Add the beaten eggs and cook for about 4 minutes, stirring all the time with a fork, until the egg is set.

9   Add the pork or chicken, a good sprinkling of soy sauce and the prawns and cook, stirring with a fork, for a further 2–3 minutes until piping hot. Serve straight away with the Chinese salad.

11 roasts and oven bakes

The good thing with oven cooking is you usually have time to go off and do something else while the meal cooks. It's worth remembering, though, that some things do require a little attention; for example, if you are roasting vegetables, in particular, they benefit from being turned over at least once during cooking so that they brown evenly.

boston ribs
with a crisp green salad

SERVES 4

storecupboard ingredients

2 x 400 g/2 x 14 oz/2 large cans of baked beans

brown table sauce

tomato ketchup (catsup)

black treacle (molasses)

dried onion granules

olive oil

wine vinegar

Dijon mustard

salt and pepper

caster (superfine) sugar

shopping list

750 g/1½ lb pork spare ribs

1 lettuce

1 cucumber

1 green (bell) pepper

1 bunch of spring onions (scallions)

1 crusty loaf

extra equipment

roasting tin (pan)

pastry brush

1   Turn on the oven to 190°C/375°F/gas mark 5.

2   Put the ribs in a single layer in the roasting tin. Place in the oven and roast for 30 minutes.

3   Mix1 tbsp brown sauce with 2 tbsp ketchup and brush over the ribs. Return them to the oven for a further 15 minutes until brown.

→   STEP 5. SEE PAGE 12

4   Remove the ribs from the tin and stir the cans of beans, a sprinkling of onion granules and 2 tbsp black treacle into the juices in the tin. Lay the ribs over the top. Cover with foil and return to the oven for 40 minutes, stirring once after 20 minutes. Put plates in the oven for the last 10 minutes to warm.

5   While the ribs are cooking, make a green salad and French dressing.   →   →

6   Spoon the ribs and beans on the warm plates and serve with crusty bread and the green salad, tossed with the French dressing.

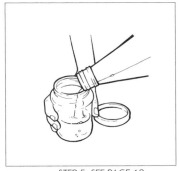

→   STEP 5. SEE PAGE 13

salmon puffs
with tomato and basil sauce

SERVES 4

storecupboard ingredients

425 g/15 oz/1 large can of pink or red salmon

215 g/7½ oz/1 small can of creamed mushrooms

375 g/13 oz frozen, ready-rolled puff pastry (paste) sheet, thawed

1 egg

pepper

passata (sieved tomatoes)

dried basil

shopping list

450 g/1 lb baby new potatoes

2 courgettes (zucchini)

2 carrots

1 lemon

extra equipment

potato peeler

baking (cookie) sheet

pastry brush

small bowl

small ovenproof dish

2 saucepans

colander

fish slice

top tip!

You can omit the creamed mushrooms and add a small spoonful of garlic and herb soft cheese to each parcel instead.

1   Cut the ends off the carrots and courgettes. Peel the carrots. Then, using a potato peeler, pare strips off both vegetables, until all of them are in ribbons. Prepare and cook the potatoes whole. ➡

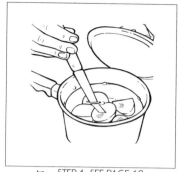

➡ STEP 1. SEE PAGE 13

2   Open the can of salmon, drain off the liquid and tip the fish on to a plate. Divide into four portions, discarding any skin and bones.

3   Put about 300 ml/½ pt/1¼ cups passata in a small ovenproof dish. Sprinkle with dried basil and a little pepper. Stir, cover with a lid or foil and put on the shelf just below the centre of the oven. Turn the oven on to 200°C/400°F/gas mark 6.

4   Cut the pastry into four squares. Put a portion of fish and a spoonful of creamed mushrooms on each. Sprinkle with pepper.

5   Break the egg into a small bowl and beat with a fork. Using a pastry brush, paint a little egg all round each square, then fold in the ends, then the sides, to seal completely.

6   Wet the baking sheet all over. Put the pastry parcels well apart on it, folded sides down. Brush all over the top of the pastry with the beaten egg.

7   Bake for about 15 minutes on the shelf above the centre of the oven until puffy and golden brown. Put plates and serving dishes into the oven to warm.

8   Boil about 2.5 cm/1 in of water in a saucepan with a pinch of salt. Add the carrot and courgette ribbons, cover with a lid and cook for 2–3 minutes until just tender. Drain in a colander, transfer to a serving dish and keep warm.

9   Check the potatoes are cooked, then drain in the colander in the sink. Put in a warm serving dish, cover with a lid and keep warm.

10 Cut the lemon into 8 wedges.

11 Put a salmon parcel and a little hot passata on each warm plate. Garnish with lemon wedges and serve with the potatoes and carrot and courgette ribbons.

toad in the hole
with sage and onion sauce and shredded savoy

SERVES 4

storecupboard ingredients

plain (all-purpose) flour

sunflower oil

dried sage

salt and pepper

dried milk powder (non-fat dry milk)

butter or margarine

milk

eggs

shopping list

450 g/1 lb thick pork sausages

1 large onion

1 small savoy cabbage

extra equipment

18 x 28 cm/7 x 11 in shallow baking tin (pan)

mixing bowl

balloon whisk

measuring jug

small saucepan

large saucepan

scissors

top tip!

To make Yorkshire puddings, heat a little oil in 12 sections of tartlet tins (patty pans) at the top of the oven at 220°C/4250F/gas mark 7. When sizzling and very hot, spoon in the batter (see right) and cook for about 20 minutes or until risen, crisp and golden.

1   Heat the oven to 220°C/425°F/gas mark 7. Pour in enough sunflower oil to cover the base of a roasting tin. Cut the sausages apart with scissors and lay them in the tin. Put in the oven to brown, while you prepare the batter.

2   Put 100 g/4 oz/1 cup plain flour in a mixing bowl and add a sprinkling of salt and pepper.

3   Pour 150 ml/¼ pt/⅔ cup milk in a measuring jug. Top up with water to 300 ml/½ pt/1¼ cups.

4   Make a hollow in the centre of the flour and break in 2 eggs. Pour in half the milk and water mixture. Whisk with a balloon whisk until smooth and creamy. Stir in the remaining milk and water.

5   Remove the baking tin from the oven and pour in the batter around the sausages. Return to the oven and cook for about 30 minutes or until puffy and golden brown.

6   While the batter is cooking, chop the onion.   ➡

➡ STEP 6. SEE PAGE 9

7   Put in the smaller saucepan and add 300 ml/½ pt/1¼ cups water and a knob of butter or margerine. Put over a high heat until the water boils, then turn down the heat to low, cover with a lid and cook for 10 minutes.

8   Using the mixing bowl you made the batter in (to save washing up!), put 3 tbsp plain flour and 3 tbsp dried milk into the bowl. Whisk in 6 tbsp water. Add a good sprinkling of dried sage and some salt and pepper. Put the plates in the oven to warm.

9   Prepare and cook the cabbage.   ➡

➡ STEP 9. SEE PAGE 10

10 Stir the blended flour and milk mixture into the cooked onions, bring to the boil and cook for 2 minutes, stirring all the time until thick.

11 When the Toad is cooked, cut into four and transfer to the warmed plates. Spoon the sage and onion sauce over and serve with the shredded cabbage.

traditional sunday roast
with all the trimmings

SERVES 4

storecupboard ingredients

sunflower oil

salt and pepper

gravy block or browning

condiments depending on roast (see chart below)

shopping list

joint or poultry (see chart below)

potatoes

carrots

parsnips

green vegetable

extra equipment

large saucepan

2 roasting tins (pans)

medium saucepan

colander

mixing bowl

measuring jug

balloon whisk

COOKING TIMES AND CONDIMENTS

Meat	Cooking time	Preparation for cooking	Condiments
beef (medium)	15 mins per 450 g/1 lb plus 15 minutes over	rub with oil, sprinkle with pepper	horseradish sauce, English mustard
beef (well-done)	20 mins per 450 g/1 lb plus 20 minutes over	rub with oil, sprinkle with pepper	horseradish sauce, English mustard
lamb	20 mins per 450 g/1 lb plus 20 minutes over	sprinkle with pepper	mint sauce or redcurrant jelly
pork	25 mins per 450 g/1 lb plus 25 minutes over	score the rind with a sharp knife in strips, rub with oil and salt, stand rind-up on an old saucer in the tin	apple sauce, sage and onion stuffing
chicken	20 mins per 450 g/1 lb plus 20 minutes over	pull off any fat round the inside edge of the body cavity, rub skin with oil and salt	bread sauce, parsley and thyme stuffing

top tips!

Before you begin, decide what time you want to eat. Work out how long the meat will take to cook (see chart above), then add on an extra 45 minutes to allow for preparation time, making the gravy and so on.

Prepare as many vegetables as you like – I usually allow 4 pieces of potatoes and 2 pieces of parsnip, an average-sized carrot and a handful of green vegetable per person.

If you want to make Yorkshire puddings, see Top Tip on page 130. To make things simpler, I suggest you buy ready-made ones which you can simply reheat while you make the gravy and dish up the vegetables.

1 Turn on the oven to 190°C/375°F/gas mark 5. Weigh the meat and calculate the cooking time, then prepare the meat for the oven (see chart opposite). Put the meat on the centre shelf and note the time it will be cooked.

2 1½ hours before the meat will be ready, put 2 tbsp oil in a roasting tin and place on a shelf near the top of the oven.

3 Prepare the potatoes and parsnips and cook together for 3 minutes only. ➡

➡ STEP 3. SEE PAGE 10

4 Strain the potatoes and parsnips in a colander over a bowl to save the cooking water for the gravy. Remove the roasting tin from the oven and add the part-cooked potatoes and parsnips. Turn over in the oil, then return to the shelf near the top of the oven.

5 If you are serving stuffing, make it up according to the packet directions. Shape into balls and arrange around the pork or chicken for the last 30 minutes of cooking time. Make up the packet of bread sauce, if appropriate.

6 Turn the potatoes and parsnips to brown the other sides.

7 When the meat is cooked, remove from the oven and transfer to a carving dish. Leave to rest while you make the gravy and cook the vegetables.

➡ STEP 7. SEE PAGE 10

8 Prepare and cook the carrots and a green leafy vegetable. Keep warm in covered dishes in the oven. Put plates, a carving dish and serving dishes, if using, to warm in the oven. ➡

9 Stir about 3 tbsp flour into the fat and juices in the roasting tin. Add about 450 ml/¾ pt/2 cups vegetable cooking water and gradually stir in until smooth. Put over a fairly high heat and cook, stirring all the time with a balloon whisk, until thickened and smooth. Add gravy block or browning and salt to taste. Thin with a little more water, if necessary.

10 Carve the meat into slices. Serve with the vegetables, gravy and chosen condiments.

nut and herb roast
with roast potatoes and cauliflower cheese

SERVES 4

storecupboard ingredients

2 slices of wholemeal bread

soy sauce

dried mixed herbs

chopped mixed nuts

sunflower oil

Marmite or Vegemite

plain (all-purpose) flour

milk

butter or margarine

Cheddar cheese

shopping list

450 g/1 lb potatoes

1 small onion

1 small cauliflower

extra equipment

roasting tin (pan)

draining spoon

colander

mixing bowl

450 g/1 lb loaf tin

large saucepan

small saucepan

balloon whisk

flameproof dish

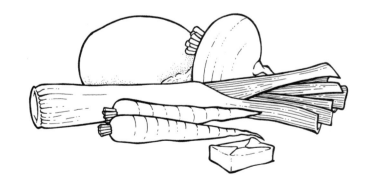

top tip!

The cauliflower cheese makes a delicious meal on its own served with crusty bread or grilled bacon rashers (slices).

1   Prepare and boil the potatoes for 3 minutes only. Lift the part-cooked potatoes out of the water and leave to drain. Leave the potato water in the pan. ➡

2   Pour about 2 tbsp oil in a roasting tin. Put in the top of the oven at 190°C/375°F/gas mark 5 until sizzling. Remove from the oven. Put the potatoes in the hot oil in the roasting tin. Return to the top shelf of the oven to cook.

➡ STEP 1. SEE PAGE 10

3   Finely chop the onion. Put in a mixing bowl. ➡

4   Break up the bread into very small pieces and add to the onion. Add 1 tbsp soy sauce, a good sprinkling of dried mixed herbs and 150 g/5 oz/1¼ cups chopped nuts.

5   Boil the kettle and measure 150 ml/¼ pt/⅔ cup boiling water in a measuring jug. Stir in 1 tsp Marmite or Vegemite and a good knob of butter or margarine until melted. Pour into the bowl and mix well, adding 1 tsp sunflower oil.

6   Brush a loaf tin with oil, then turn the mixture into the tin and press down well. Bake on the centre shelf of the oven for 40 minutes until crisp on top and hot through.

➡ STEP 3. SEE PAGE 9

7   While the nut roast cooks, cut the cauliflower into florets, discarding the thick central stalk. Bring the potato water to the boil again and cook the cauliflower for about 5 minutes until tender. Drain in a colander in the sink, then put in an ovenproof dish.

8   Make a basic white sauce. Grate some Cheddar cheese until you have a good handful. Stir most of it into the sauce and pour over the cauliflower. Sprinkle with the remaining cheese. Turn on the grill (broiler). Put the cauliflower cheese under the grill for about 5 minutes until golden on top and bubbling. Put plates to warm, either under the grill or in the oven. ➡

9   Loosen the edge of the nut roast with a round-bladed knife, then turn out on to a warm dish. Cut into slices and serve with the roast potatoes and cauliflower cheese.

➡ STEP 8. SEE PAGE 14

shepherd's pie
with golden cheesy topping

SERVES 4

storecupboard ingredients

1 beef or chicken stock cube

dried mixed herbs

salt and pepper

plain (all-purpose) flour

frozen peas

butter or margarine

milk

Cheddar cheese

shopping list

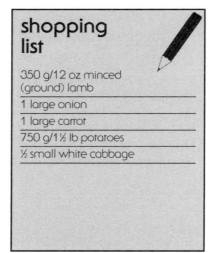

350 g/12 oz minced (ground) lamb

1 large onion

1 large carrot

750 g/1½ lb potatoes

½ small white cabbage

extra equipment

2 large saucepans

potato masher

grater

measuring jug

colander

fairly large flameproof dish

top tip!

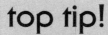

You can prepare the pie earlier in the day, then cool completely and store in the fridge until required. Cook in the oven at 190°C/375°F/gas mark 5 for about 35 minutes until bubbling and golden brown, instead of browning under the grill (broiler).

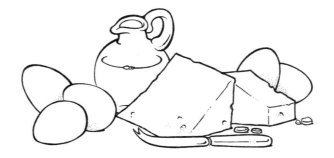

1 Chop the onion and dice the carrot. ➡ ➡

2 Cut the hard V-shaped core out of the cabbage, then grate the cabbage on the coarse side of a grater.

3 Prepare and boil the potatoes. ➡

➡ STEP 1. SEE PAGE 9

4 As soon as you have put the potatoes on the heat, put the lamb in a saucepan with the chopped onion and carrot. Cook over a fairly high heat, stirring all the time with a wooden spoon until the meat is no longer pink and all the grains are separate.

5 Add enough water to cover the meat, then crumble in the stock cube and stir. Add the cabbage and stir. Season well with salt and pepper and add a good sprinkling of dried mixed herbs. Cover with a lid and heat until the mixture is bubbling rapidly. Turn down the heat to fairly low and let it bubble gently for 20 minutes.

6 When the potatoes are tender, tip into a colander in the sink to drain, then tip the potatoes back in the saucepan.

➡ STEP 1. SEE PAGE 10

7 Add a good knob of butter or margarine and a splash of milk and mash thoroughly with a potato masher. Add a little more milk, if you like, but don't make it too soft.

8 Grate some Cheddar cheese to make a small handful.

9 Add a handful of frozen peas to the meat mixture. Mix 3 tbsp flour with 4 tbsp water in a cup until smooth. Stir into the meat mixture and cook for a further 2 minutes, stirring until thickened. Taste and add more seasoning, if necessary.

10 Turn on the grill (broiler) and put plates under to warm. Spoon the meat mixture into a flameproof dish. Top with spoonfuls of the mashed potato, then very lightly spread it out over the top to cover completely, using a fork.

➡ STEP 3. SEE PAGE 10

11 Sprinkle the cheese over the potato. Put under the hot grill for a few minutes until the cheese has melted and the top is turning golden brown. Serve hot.

marmalade-glazed bacon
with winter vegetables

SERVES 4

storecupboard ingredients

caster (superfine) sugar

orange marmalade

salt and pepper

1 bay leaf

English or Dijon mustard

shopping list

1.5 kg/3 lb unsmoked bacon joint

4 onions

4 potatoes

4 carrots

1 bunch of watercress

extra equipment

large saucepan

draining spoon

2 roasting tins (pans)

carving knife and fork

measuring jug

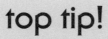

top tip!

Any bacon joint left over will be delicious cold with a mixed salad (see page 12) and chips (fries) (see page 11) or new potatoes (see page 10).

1   Put the bacon joint in a large saucepan and cover with cold water. Add the bay leaf. Cover with a lid and place over a high heat until it boils. Take off the lid and use a draining spoon to skim off as much of the white scum from the surface as you can.

2   Turn down the heat until the water is only very gently bubbling. Cover again and leave to cook for 40 minutes while you prepare the vegetables.

3   Peel the onions but leave whole. Prepare and cut the potatoes and carrots into large chunks. ➡

➡ STEP 3. SEE PAGE 10

4   When the meat has been cooking for 40 minutes, add the vegetables all round the joint and cook for a further 10 minutes.

5   Turn on the oven to 190°C/375°F/gas mark 5. Carefully lift out the vegetables with a draining spoon and place in a roasting tin. Add 6 tbsp cooking water. Sprinkle all over with 2 tbsp caster sugar and a little salt and pepper. Lift out the meat and place in another tin. Leave until it is cool enough to touch, then carefully pull or cut off any rind and smear the surface with 2 tbsp orange marmalade.

6   Measure about 450 ml/¾ pt/2 cups of the cooking water and pour round the joint.

7   Put the vegetables on the top shelf of the oven and the meat underneath. Cook for about 40 minutes until the meat and vegetables are golden brown. Twice during cooking, tilt the vegetable tin and spoon some of the liquid over the vegetables to keep them moist.

8   While the meal is cooking, put the plates and a carving dish in the oven to warm. Trim the ends off the watercress stalks, rinse and pat dry on kitchen paper (paper towels).

9   Transfer the cooked bacon to the warm carving dish. Cut as much as you need into slices. Transfer to the warm plates and spoon some of the cooking juices from the meat tin over. Add the vegetables, garnish with watercress and serve with mustard.

greek lamb
with village salad

SERVES 4

storecupboard ingredients

garlic purée (paste)

1 chicken stock cube

dried oregano

salt and pepper

olive oil

red wine vinegar

shopping list

½ leg of lamb, about 1.25 kg/2½ lb

8 potatoes

1 lettuce

2 tomatoes

1 cucumber

1 onion

fresh parsley

1 small jar or can of black olives

100 g/4 oz Feta cheese

extra equipment

large roaster baster or flameproof casserole dish (Dutch oven)

salad bowl

carving dish

scissors

carving knife and fork

1   Turn on the oven to 160°C/325°F/gas mark 3. Put the lamb in a large roaster baster or flameproof casserole dish.

2   Peel and cut the potatoes into very large pieces. Arrange around the meat.

3   Put a squeeze of garlic purée on the skin of the lamb and rub all over. Sprinkle with pepper and dried oregano.

4   Pour enough water around the meat to come about 1 cm/½ in up the sides. Sprinkle the potatoes with salt. Crumble the stock cube into the water.

5   Cover with a lid and cook in the oven for 4 hours. At the end of the cooking time, put plates and a carving dish in to warm.

6   While the lamb cooks, prepare a mixed salad. Top with a few olives. Cut the cheese into crumbly cubes and scatter over. Sprinkle with a little dried oregano and salt and pepper. Trickle about 3 tbsp olive oil and 1 tbsp wine vinegar over.   ➡

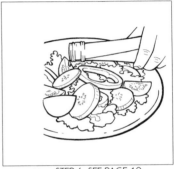

➡ STEP 6. SEE PAGE 12

7   Transfer the lamb and potatoes to the carving dish. Chop the parsley (see Top Tip page 20).

8   Put the pan of cooking liquid on the hob over a high heat and boil, stirring, for 2–3 minutes until it is slightly reduced in quantity and thickened.

9   Cut all the meat off the bones and place on plates with the potatoes. Spoon the liquid over and sprinkle with chopped parsley. Serve with the village salad.

moussaka
with cabbage and carrot vinaigrette

SERVES 4

storecupboard ingredients

garlic purée (paste)

tomato purée

1 beef stock cube

salt and pepper

ground cinnamon

dried oregano

olive oil

white wine vinegar

1 egg

Cheddar cheese

shopping list

350 g/12 oz minced (ground) beef or lamb

1 onion

1 large aubergine (eggplant)

½ small white cabbage

2 carrots

1 small carton of plain yoghurt

extra equipment

large saucepan

medium saucepan

measuring jug

colander

grater

large ovenproof dish

salad bowl

top tip!

If you don't like aubergine, use 2 large courgettes (zucchini) or potatoes instead.

1   Chop the onion.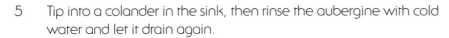

2   Put in a large saucepan with the minced meat. Cook over a fairly high heat, stirring, until the meat is no longer pink and all the grains are separate.

3   Add 300 ml/½ pt/1¼ cups water. Crumble in the stock cube and add a small squeeze of garlic purée and a good squeeze of tomato purée. Stir well. Sprinkle a little salt and pepper, dried oregano and ground cinnamon over the surface and stir in. Heat until the mixture boils rapidly, then turn the heat down to moderate and let it bubble gently for 15 minutes, stirring occasionally.

STEP 1. SEE PAGE 9

4   Meanwhile, slice the aubergine, discarding the stalk end. Put about 1 cm/½ in water in a medium saucepan and let it come to the boil. Add the aubergine slices and boil for about 4 minutes until tender.

5   Tip into a colander in the sink, then rinse the aubergine with cold water and let it drain again.

6   Layer the meat mixture and aubergine slices in an ovenproof dish, finishing with a layer of aubergine.

7   Turn on the oven to 190°C/375°F/gas mark 5. Grate enough Cheddar cheese on the coarse side of the grater to make a large handful.

8   Break an egg into a bowl and whisk in the yoghurt and a sprinkling of salt and pepper. Stir in the cheese.

9   Spoon over the aubergine and bake in the oven for 40 minutes until the top is set and golden brown. Put plates in to warm towards the end of the cooking time.

10 While the moussaka is cooking, cut the thick central stalk out of the cabbage and peel the carrots, cutting off all the ends. Grate the cabbage and carrots on the coarse side of a grater. Put in a salad bowl. Sprinkle with about 3 tbsp olive oil, 1 tbsp vinegar and a little salt and pepper. Stir well. Serve with the moussaka.

italian-style pork
with mozzarella potatoes and green salad

SERVES 4

storecupboard ingredients

298 g/10¾ oz/1 medium can of condensed cream of tomato soup

olive oil

salt and pepper

dried onion granules

dried basil

red wine vinegar

caster (superfine) sugar

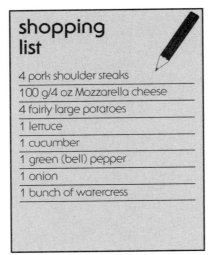

shopping list

4 pork shoulder steaks

100 g/4 oz Mozzarella cheese

4 fairly large potatoes

1 lettuce

1 cucumber

1 green (bell) pepper

1 onion

1 bunch of watercress

extra equipment

flameproof casserole (Dutch oven)

2 metal skewers

grater

salad bowl

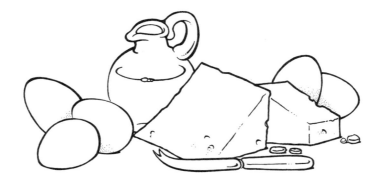

top tip!
This dish is also delicious made with lamb steaks or chops.

1   Scrub the potatoes and prick all over with a fork. Thread two on each of two skewers and place in the oven at 160°C/325°F/gas mark 3.

2   Heat 1 tbsp oil in a flameproof casserole over a high heat. Add the pork and brown on both sides. Pour off any remaining oil. Sprinkle with a little dried onion.

3   Spoon the can of soup over the pork and sprinkle with dried basil, salt and pepper.

4   Cover with a lid and place in the oven with the potatoes. Cook for 1½ hours.

5   While the potatoes and pork cook, make a green salad and French dressing. ➡ ➡

6   Grate the Mozzarella cheese. Put the plates in the oven to warm.

7   Remove the potatoes from the skewers. Make a large cross-cut in each and squeeze to open slightly.

8   Transfer the potatoes to the warm plates. Put the cheese on top and sprinkle with dried basil. Spoon the pork on to the plates, stir the sauce and spoon over. Serve with the green salad separately.

➡ STEP 5. SEE PAGE 12

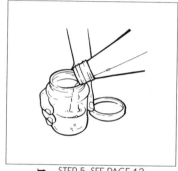

➡ STEP 5. SEE PAGE 13

12 easy entertaining

Planning a supper party can be tricky. But this chapter takes away all the hassle. I have chosen main meals from other chapters and teamed them up with the ideal, simple starter and dessert to create stylish three-course meals with very little effort. The instructions tell you exactly when and how to prepare everything so you can sit down with your guests and enjoy the party.

menu 1
guacamole with tortilla chips
chilli con carne with rice*
ice cream with hot chocolate sauce

SERVES 4

storecupboard ingredients

lemon juice

garlic purée (paste)

chilli powder

paprika

Worcestershire sauce

olive oil

toasted chopped nuts

milk

butter or margarine

vanilla ice cream

shopping list

2 ripe avocados

tortilla chips

2 Mars bars

extra equipment

mixing bowl

small balloon whisk or fork

small saucepan

* see page 96 for ingredients and equipment

1 Make the chilli earlier in the day or at least 3 hours before you want to serve the meal. Cover with a saucepan lid and leave to cool. Do the same with the rice: simply cook and drain and leave in a colander, covered with a saucepan lid. If made so long in advance it gets completely cold, then store it in the fridge. Prepare the garnishes for the main course, cover them with clingfilm (plastic wrap) and store in the fridge.

2 You can make the guacamole up to 2 hours before serving (no longer or it will discolour). Cut the avocados into halves, remove the stones, then scoop the flesh out into a bowl.

3 Mash with a fork or small balloon whisk, adding a good dash of lemon juice.

4 Add a small squeeze of garlic purée, a good pinch of chilli powder and a sprinkling of Worcestershire sauce. Gradually whisk in 6 tbsp oil, a very little at a time, until the mixture is creamy. Taste and add more chilli or Worcestershire sauce, if liked.

5 Cover the bowl with clingfilm (plastic wrap) and chill in the fridge.

6 Now make the chocolate sauce: break up the Mars bars and put them in a saucepan. Add about 4 tbsp milk and a knob of butter or margarine. Heat over a gentle heat, stirring until the mixture melts and is smooth. Add a little more milk, if liked. Put to one side ready to reheat before serving.

7 About 20 minutes before you want to eat, reheat the rice and chilli. Half-fill the rice saucepan with hot water, put the colander of rice covered with the saucepan lid over the top and put over a high heat. As soon as the water is bubbling and steam is rising through the rice, turn the heat down as low as possible. Reheat the chilli over a moderate heat, stirring until bubbling, then turn down as low as possible and cover with a saucepan lid. Put plates on top to warm.

8 Spoon the guacamole into small pots. Sprinkle with a little paprika and place on individual serving plates. Surround with tortilla chips and serve.

9 For the main course, stir the chilli, fork through the rice and serve.

10 When ready to serve dessert, reheat the chocolate sauce, stirring until hot and smooth. Put scoops of ice cream into individual dishes, spoon the sauce over, sprinkle with chopped nuts and serve.

top tip!

To tell if avocados are ripe, the shiny, green-skinned ones should feel slightly soft when gently squeezed in the palm of your hand. The knobbly-skinned ones should be black on the outside but should not feel soft.

menu 2

brandied pâté with toast

chicken in red wine with sesame seed potatoes and mangetout*

mediterranean fresh fruit with raspberry coulis

SERVES 4–6

storecupboard ingredients

butter

brandy

sliced bread

salt and pepper

shopping list
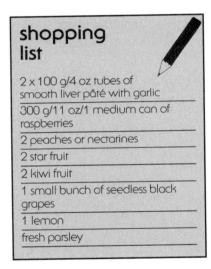

2 x 100 g/4 oz tubes of smooth liver pâté with garlic

300 g/11 oz/1 medium can of raspberries

2 peaches or nectarines

2 star fruit

2 kiwi fruit

1 small bunch of seedless black grapes

1 lemon

fresh parsley

extra equipment

small saucepan

mixing bowl

small bowl

food processor or blender (optional)

sieve (strainer)

large plastic container with lid

* see page 100 for ingredients and equipment

1   Start the preparation at least 4 hours before you want to serve.

2   First, make the pâté. Melt 75 g/3 oz/⅓ cup butter in a saucepan over a gentle heat.

3   Scoop the liver pâté into a mixing bowl. Add about half the melted butter and a good splash of brandy and mash well with a wooden spoon until well blended. Taste and add salt and pepper.

4   Spoon into a small dish, smooth over the surface, then pour over the remaining butter. Chill in the fridge until ready to serve.

5   Now, make the raspberry coulis. Put a sieve over a bowl, empty the raspberries into the sieve and rub through with a wooden spoon. Scrape off any purée sticking to the base of the sieve, then discard the seeds. Alternatively, purée the raspberries and juice in a blender or food processor, then rub through the sieve to remove the seeds. Chill until ready to serve.

6   Cut the peaches into halves, remove the stones (pits), then cut into neat slices. Place in a plastic container with a lid. Slice the star fruit, so each slice looks like a star. Place in the container. Cut off the stalk ends from the kiwi fruit, peel off the skin, then cut into slices. Place in the container. Halve the grapes and put in the container. Put the lid on the container and chill.

7   Prepare and cook the chicken in red wine and sesame seed potatoes (see page 101). When they are cooked, you can turn the oven down to very low until ready to serve. Don't cook the mangetout until you have served the starter.

8   About 15 minutes before you wish to serve the starter, put plates to warm.

9   Make one or two slices of toast per person. Cut into triangles. Spoon the brandied pâté on to four or six small plates. Cut the lemon into wedges and put one on each plate with a sprig of parsley. Add the toast and serve.

10 After the starter, cook the mangetout (see page 101). Serve with the chicken and potatoes.

11 After the main course, spoon the raspberry coulis on four or six dessert plates to form a pool over the base of the plate. Arrange the fruits attractively on top and serve.

top tip!

For the dessert, you can use any selection of fresh fruit you like. Leave on any edible skin for added colour and texture.

menu 3

chilled carrot, tomato and orange soup
grilled salmon fillets with hollandaise sauce, new potatoes and salad*
chocolate rum cups

SERVES 4

storecupboard ingredients

275 g/10 oz/1 medium can of carrots

400 g/14 oz/1 large can of tomatoes

pure orange juice

dried basil

salt and pepper

rum

toasted chopped nuts

shopping list

284 ml/10 fl oz/1 medium carton of double (heavy) or whipping cream

1 packet of ready-made chocolate cases

1 jar of chocolate and hazelnut spread

100 g/4 oz strawberries

extra equipment

blender or food processor

plastic container with lid

mixing bowl

electric or balloon whisk

* see page 60 for ingredients and equipment

1. Make the soup and dessert well in advance. Make the soup first. Drain the liquid from the can of carrots and tip them into a blender or food processor with the contents of the can of tomatoes. Run the machine until smooth.

2. Add 150 ml/¼ pt/⅔ cup orange juice, a good sprinkling of basil and a small sprinkling of salt and pepper. Blend briefly again.

3. Pour into a plastic container with a lid and chill until ready to serve.

4. To make the chocolate cups, pour a good half of the cream into a bowl. Whisk with an electric or balloon whisk until stiff.

5. Add 2 tbsp chocolate spread (be generous!) and gently stir in with 1 tbsp rum.

6. Spoon this mixture into four or six ready-made chocolate cases but leave them sitting in their container. Swirl the top of the chocolate cream gently with a teaspoon and sprinkle with a few toasted, chopped nuts. Chill until ready to serve.

7. Prepare the main course (see page 61). Just before your guests arrive, cook the potatoes but don't grill (broil) the fish. Keep the potatoes warm in a serving dish in the oven at the lowest setting.

8. When you are ready to serve the meal, lay the fish on the grill (broiler) rack but do not cook yet. Ladle the soup into soup bowls. Serve with 1 tsp cream swirled over the centre of each portion.

9. After the starter has been eaten, grill the fish, then serve the main course (see page 61).

10. When your guests are ready for the dessert, put the chocolate cups on small plates. Arrange two or three whole strawberries to one side and serve.

top tip!

When you make the chocolate cups, you can substitute brandy, whisky or coffee liqueur for the rum – or leave it out altogether if you prefer.

menu 4

creamed garlic mussels

oregano lemon chicken on a vegetable platter*

strawberry shortcakes

SERVES 4–6

storecupboard ingredients

butter or margarine

garlic purée (paste)

white wine

cornflour (cornstarch)

pepper

caster (superfine) sugar

vanilla essence (extract)

shopping list

2 cans of mussels in brine (NOT vinegar)

284 g/10 fl oz/1 medium carton of double (heavy) or whipping cream

1 onion

fresh parsley

100 g/4 oz small strawberries

1 packet of round shortcake biscuits (cookies)

1 stick of French bread

extra equipment

saucepan

wineglass

scissors

electric or balloon whisk

* see page 58 for ingredients and equipment

1   Earlier in the day or at least 2 hours before you want to serve the meal, you can prepare the chicken and vegetables for cooking (see page 59) and prepare the starter ready to heat through before serving. Chop the onion (see page 9).

2   Melt a knob of butter or margarine in a saucepan over a moderate heat. Add the onion and cook, stirring, for 2 minutes until soft but not brown. Add two small squeezes of garlic purée. Remove from the heat.

3   Drain the liquid from one of the cans of mussels into the onion. Drain off the liquid from the other can. Add a wineglass of white wine to the onion in the saucepan. Put 1 tbsp cornflour in a cup, measure a wineglass of water and mix a little of it into the cornflour until smooth. Stir this mixture into the saucepan with the rest of the water.

4   Heat the mixture until it boils, stirring all the time until thickened and smooth. Remove from the heat and stir in half the carton of cream. Chop a small handful of parsley (see Top Tip page 20). Add half of it to the sauce. Season to taste and leave to cool.

5   Whip the remaining cream with 1 tbsp caster sugar and a few drops of vanilla essence, using an electric or balloon whisk. Chill until ready to serve.

6   At least 30 minutes before you want to eat, cook the chicken and vegetables. Keep them warm in a low oven. Finish preparing the starter. Put some soup bowls and the French bread in the oven to warm.

7   Put the mussels in the sauce. Stir over a high heat until bubbling. Cook for 2 minutes. Spoon into the warmed soup bowls. Sprinkle with the remaining chopped parsley and serve with the French bread.

8   Serve the main course (see page 59).

9   Once the main course is finished, put a shortcake biscuit on each of four or six small plates. Pile on some cream. Top with strawberries and a dusting of caster sugar and serve.

menu 5

greek dips with pitta bread
moussaka with cabbage and carrot vinaigrette*
Athenian figs

SERVES 4

storecupboard ingredients

dried mint

olive oil

clear honey

shopping list

1 jar of black olives

415 g/14½ oz/1 large can of green figs in syrup

250 g/9 oz/1 medium tub of hummus

250 g/9 oz/1 medium tub of tzatziki

250 g/9 oz/1 medium tub of taramasalata

450 ml/¾ pt/2 cups Greek-style natural yoghurt

1 packet of pitta breads

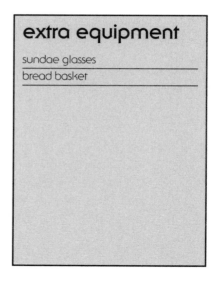

extra equipment

sundae glasses

bread basket

* see page 142 for ingredients and equipment

1   Prepare the moussaka and salad (see page 143).

2   While the moussaka is cooking, open the can of figs and cut each fruit into quarters. Divide among the sundae glasses and pour in enough of the juice just to cover the fruit.

3   Spoon the yoghurt on top, then cover completely with a layer of clear honey. Chill until ready to serve.

4   When you are nearly ready to dish up, put the pitta breads to warm: either wrap them in foil and put in the base of the oven or place briefly under the grill (broiler). Put a spoonful of each of the three dips on individual plates. Put a small pile of black olives in the centre of each plate. Drizzle a little olive oil over the taramasalata and hummus. Sprinkle the tzatziki with dried mint.

5   Cut the pitta bread into fingers and put in a bread basket. Serve the starter.

6   Serve the main course.

7   Serve the dessert, straight from the fridge.

top tip!

The moussaka can be made in advance up to step 9 (see page 143), ready to cook as your guests are due to arrive.

menu 6

cheesy tuna pots

grilled pork chops with peaches, new potatoes and green beans*

blackcurrant mousse

SERVES 4

storecupboard ingredients

170 g/6 oz/1 small can of evaporated milk

300 g/11 oz/1 medium can of blackcurrants

185 g/6½ oz/1 small can of tuna

lemon juice

cayenne

salt and pepper

paprika

sliced bread

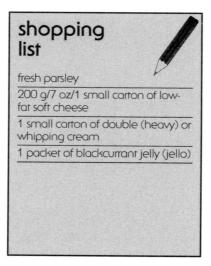

shopping list

fresh parsley

200 g/7 oz/1 small carton of low-fat soft cheese

1 small carton of double (heavy) or whipping cream

1 packet of blackcurrant jelly (jello)

extra equipment

2 bowls

electric or balloon whisk

measuring jug

glass serving dish

scissors

4 small ramekins (custard cups)

* see page 54 for ingredients and equipment

1   Put the evaporated milk in the fridge to chill for at least 2 hours.

2   Boil the kettle and pour 150 ml/¼ pt/⅔ cup boiling water in the measuring jug. Break up the jelly, add to the water and stir until dissolved.

3   Open the can of blackcurrants and pour off the juice into the jelly mixture. Stir well and place in the fridge until it has set to the consistency of egg white.

4   Pour the chilled evaporated milk into a bowl and whisk until thick and fluffy. Whisk in the almost-setting jelly. Spoon into a glass serving dish and chill until set.

5   Now make the starter. Drain the liquid from the can of tuna and empty the fish into a bowl. Mash with a fork, then mash in the cheese until well blended. Add a good dash of lemon juice and a generous pinch of cayenne, then season to taste with salt and pepper.

6   Chop a sprig of parsley (see Top Tip page 20). Spoon the tuna mixture into four small ramekins. Sprinkle with paprika and the parsley and cover with clingfilm (plastic wrap). Chill until you are ready to serve.

7   Whip the cream until just stiff and spread over the set blackcurrant mousse. Return to the fridge. Drain the blackcurrants on kitchen paper (paper towels) and keep on one side.

8   Prepare and cook the main course (see page 55). Keep warm in a low oven. Put the plates for the main course in to warm.

9   About 10 minutes before you want to serve the meal, make one or two slices of toast per person and cut into fingers. Put a pot of tuna cheese on each of four individual plates and put the fingers of toast to one side. Remove the clingfilm and serve.

10 Serve the main course.

11 After the main course, pile the blackcurrants in the centre of the cream on the mousse and serve.

top tip!

You need to allow several hours for chilling and setting time for the dessert. To be on the safe side, prepare the starter and the dessert up to a day before, then chill until ready to serve.

menu 7

consommé with mushrooms
trout with almonds, baby new potatoes and mangetout*
chocolate and lemon flan

SERVES 4

storecupboard ingredients

200 g/7 oz/1 small can of sweetened condensed milk

lemon juice

sherry

butter

shopping list

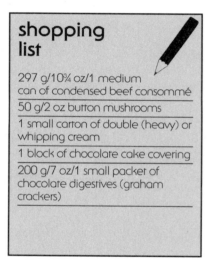

297 g/10¾ oz/1 medium can of condensed beef consommé

50 g/2 oz button mushrooms

1 small carton of double (heavy) or whipping cream

1 block of chocolate cake covering

200 g/7 oz/1 small packet of chocolate digestives (graham crackers)

extra equipment

plastic bag

rolling pin

saucepan

20 cm/8 in flan dish (pie pan)

mixing bowl

whisk

electric or balloon whisk

grater

* see page 34 for ingredients and equipment

1   First, make the flan. If you have not prepared it in advance, start at least 4 hours before you want to eat, to allow it to chill. Empty the digestives into a plastic bag. Crush with a rolling pin.

2   Melt 50 g/2 oz/¼ cup butter in a saucepan over a gentle heat. Remove from the heat and stir in the biscuits. Press into the base and sides of a flan dish, then chill in the fridge to set.

3   Empty the cream into a bowl and whip until it stands in soft peaks but is not too stiff. Stir in the condensed milk and 6 tbsp lemon juice. Spoon into the flan case (pie shell) and chill again.

4   Wipe the mushrooms to remove any soil. Slice thinly. Rinse out the biscuit crumb saucepan. Add the mushrooms and 2 tbsp water. Cook, stirring, over a moderate heat for 2 minutes until the mushrooms have softened. Stir in the consommé and a canful of water. Add a good slosh of sherry. Leave ready to reheat just before serving.

5   Prepare the main course (see page 35).

6   Once your guests have arrived, cook the main course (see page 35). Cover the fish with foil, put the vegetables in serving dishes and keep warm in a very low oven. Put soup bowls and plates in to warm.

7   Heat the soup until almost boiling. Ladle into the soup bowls and serve very hot.

8   Serve the main course.

9   Grate a little chocolate cake covering over the flan and serve.

top tip!
If you like, you can make the dessert the day before to allow time for it to chill and set. The soup can also be prepared earlier in the day, ready to reheat at the last moment.

menu 8

smoked mackerel with horseradish mayonnaise

marmalade-glazed bacon with winter vegetables*

melon with minted raspberries

SERVES 6

storecupboard ingredients

horseradish sauce or relish

good-quality mayonnaise

caster (superfine) sugar

sliced brown bread

butter

shopping list

6 smoked mackerel fillers

3 small, ripe ogen or chanterais melons

225 g/8 oz raspberries

1 lemon

fresh mint

fresh parsley

extra equipment

scissors

small mixing bowl

* see page 138 for ingredients and equipment

1   Start your preparation at least 2½ hours before you plan to eat. Cut the melons into halves and scoop out the seeds. Wrap and chill until ready to serve.

2   Chop a small handful of mint (see Top Tip page 20). Stir in 2 tbsp caster sugar.

3   Remove any stalks from the raspberries and put the fruit in a container. Sprinkle the minted sugar over and toss very gently with a spoon or your hands, to coat. Cover and chill until ready to serve.

4   At least 2 hours before you wish to serve, prepare and cook the main course (see page 139).

5   While it is cooking, butter one or two slices of bread per person and cut into triangles. Place on a serving plate and cover with clingfilm (plastic wrap) until ready to serve.

6   Mix 1 tbsp horseradish sauce or relish with 6 tbsp mayonnaise. Season to taste with pepper. Chill.

7   Carve the meat, cover with foil and put back in a low oven to keep warm together with the plates and the vegetables, also in covered dishes.

8   When ready to serve, lay a mackerel fillet on each of six individual dishes. Spoon a little of the horseradish mayonnaise to one side. Cut the lemon into six wedges. Put a wedge of lemon and a small sprig of parsley on each plate. Serve.

9   Serve the main course.

10 When ready to serve the dessert, put the melon halves in six individual dishes. Pile the raspberries in the centre and decorate each with small sprig of mint. Serve.

top tip!

You can prepare the main course as far as step 6 earlier in the day, but don't turn on the oven. Just before your guests are due to arrive, heat the oven, put in the joint and vegetables and complete the cooking. You can also prepare the dessert up to step 3 well in advance.

menu 9
grilled grapefruit with port
flashy piquant steaks with sauté potatoes and broccoli*
apricot cheesecake

SERVES 4

storecupboard ingredients

caster (superfine) sugar

vanilla essence (extract)

light brown sugar

port

shopping list
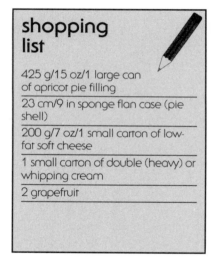

425 g/15 oz/1 large can of apricot pie filling

23 cm/9 in sponge flan case (pie shell)

200 g/7 oz/1 small carton of low-fat soft cheese

1 small carton of double (heavy) or whipping cream

2 grapefruit

extra equipment

serving plate

2 mixing bowls

electric or balloon whisk

serrated edged grapefruit knife

* see page 36 for ingredients and equipment

1   Make the dessert at least 4 hours before you plan to eat, or even the day before, so it has time to chill. Put the flan case on a serving plate. Whip the cream until it stands in soft peaks.

2   Put the cheese in a separate bowl and stir in 4 tbsp caster sugar and a few drops of vanilla essence. Using a metal tablespoon, fold in the whipped cream.

3   Spoon the mixture into the flan case and smooth the surface. Chill in the fridge to set.

4   Now make the starter, also well in advance. Cut the grapefruit in halves through the middle. Using a serrated grapefruit knife, cut all round the edge of each between the pith and the flesh, then separate each segment from the side of each membrane and loosen the segments. Put in four flameproof individual dishes. Pour a spoonful of port over each and sprinkle liberally with light brown sugar.

5   Spoon the apricot pie filling over the cheesecake and return to the fridge until ready to serve.

6   Just before your guests arrive – or ideally, while they are enjoying a pre-dinner drink, – cook the main course (see page 37). Keep the sauté potatoes warm in a low oven. Put the cooked broccoli in the colander over the saucepan and cover with the saucepan lid to keep warm on top of the stove. Cook the steaks, cover and keep warm in the oven, but don't make the sauce yet.

7   Turn on the grill (broiler). Put the grapefruit under the grill until the sugar melts and caramelises. Serve straight away.

8   When the grapefruit have been eaten, quickly cook the onion and finish the sauce for the steaks. Put the steaks on warm plates, spoon the sauce over and serve with the vegetables.

9   Finally, serve the dessert, cut into slices.

top tip!

If you prefer not to have the trouble of cooking sauté potatoes when you have guests, cook baby new potatoes (see page 10), which can be kept warm in their saucepan or can cook gently while you are serving the starter.

menu 10
pears with blue cheese dressing
spiced persian lamb with flageolets*
raspberry and yoghurt ruffle

SERVES 6

storecupboard ingredients

550g/1¼ lb/1 very large can of pear halves

good-quality mayonnaise

lemon juice

paprika

light brown sugar

milk

pure orange juice

shopping list

1 packet of trifle sponges

300 g/11 oz/1 medium can of raspberries

284 ml/10 fl oz/1 medium carton of double (heavy) cream

1 small carton of vanilla-flavoured yoghurt

100 g/4 oz Danish blue cheese

1 lettuce

extra equipment

2 small bowls

electric or balloon whisk

large glass serving bowl

* see page 82 for ingredients and equipment

1   Marinate the lamb (see page 82).

2   Make the dessert. Crumble four trifle sponges into a glass serving dish. Open the can of raspberries and pour into the dish. Mash well so the sponges soak up the juice. Add enough orange juice to soak the sponges completely and stir well.

3   Whip the yoghurt and all but about 4 tbsp of the cream together until the mixture is just standing in soft peaks. Spoon over the raspberry mixture. Sprinkle liberally with light brown sugar and chill for several hours, or overnight, so the sugar melts.

4   Finish preparing the lamb and cook to step 8 (see page 83). Once it is cooked, turn down the oven as low as possible and leave it ready to be sliced when you want to serve.

5   Make the dressing for the pears. Cut off any rind from the blue cheese and place the cheese in a bowl. Crush with a fork. Using a wooden spoon or whisk, beat in the reserved cream, 4 tbsp mayonnaise and a dash of lemon juice. Thin with a little milk, if necessary, so the mixture will coat the back of a spoon.

6   Just before your guests arrive, drain the pears. Put lettuce leaves on individual plates and put two pear halves on each plate. Spoon the blue cheese mayonnaise over. Sprinkle with paprika. Chill, if liked, until ready to serve.

7   Cut up the lamb and thicken the vegetables (see page 83). Cover the lamb and potatoes with foil and return to the oven to keep warm. Put in plates to warm. Turn off the heat under the vegetables.

8   Serve the starter.

9   Reheat the thickened vegetables and serve the main course (see page 83).

10   Serve the dessert.

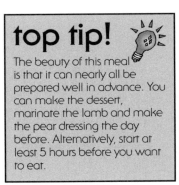

top tip!

The beauty of this meal is that it can nearly all be prepared well in advance. You can make the dessert, marinate the lamb and make the pear dressing the day before. Alternatively, start at least 5 hours before you want to eat.

index